God or Bust

How to Keep the Faith When Life Knocks You Down

Elijah Singer
with
Jason C. Johnson Sr.

One Plan Media LLC

Copyright © 2024 by One Plan Media LLC

All rights reserved.

No portion of this book may be reproduced in any form without written permission from the publisher or author, except as permitted by U.S. copyright law.

"Scripture quotations are from The ESV® Bible (The Holy Bible, English Standard Version®), © 2001 by Crossway, a publishing ministry of Good News Publishers. Used by permission. All rights reserved."

Although the author and publisher have made every effort to ensure that the information in this book was correct at press time, the author and publisher do not assume and hereby disclaim any liability to any party for any loss, damage, or disruption caused by errors or omissions, whether such errors or omissions result from negligence, accident, or any other cause.

Adherence to all applicable laws and regulations, including international, federal, state and local governing professional licensing, business practices, advertising, and all other aspects of doing business in the US, Canada or any other jurisdiction is the sole responsibility of the reader and consumer.

Neither the author nor the publisher assumes any responsibility or liability whatsoever on behalf of the consumer or reader of this material. Any perceived slight of any individual or organization is purely unintentional.

The resources in this book are provided for informational purposes only and should not be used to replace the specialized training and professional judgment of a health care or mental health care professional.

Neither the author nor the publisher can be held responsible for the use of the information provided within this book. Please always consult a trained professional before making any decision regarding treatment of yourself or others.

Contents

Author's Note	1
Introduction	5
The Meaning of Trusting God	
1. Life Won't Let Me Trust	11
2. God, Where are You?	23
3. Why Don't You Care?	31
4. Habakkuk's Queries	37
5. Won't You Take Action?	43
6. It Seems Unfair	51
7. A Crisis of Faith	57
8. Lost and Found	69
9. Put it in Writing	81
10. Wait Patiently	89
11. By Faith	95
12. Faith Tested	101
13. Remember	107
14. Accept	117

15. Trust	123
16. Hope	129
17. Believe	135
Ahem...	139
Conclusion To Doubt or to Believe?	141
References	149
Next Read	151
About the Publisher	153

GOD Or BUST

HOW TO KEEP THE FAITH WHEN LIFE KNOCKS YOU DOWN

ELIJAH SINGER

WITH JASON C. JOHNSON SR.

Author's Note

I consider Laura Collins to be family. She is the friendliest, effervescent, outgoing, and enjoyable person I know. She has worked in my office for years, and I love her and her family.

She bounded into my office one day many years ago, gleaming with joy. She was shouting and dancing simultaneously, barely managing to speak. She was expecting a child with her husband, Benjamin. We had prayed for it, and it came to pass. But we followed the same procedure when she miscarried. Only the feelings were so profoundly different.

As a pastor, I see a lot of loss. It's never simple, especially if a close friend or family member is involved. And we conducted the standard practice of *God, why did you allow this to occur?*

I began writing this book at that time. I typed, wrote, and continued to write. And I kept my writing to myself. I wrote with Laura in mind at all times, but I knew Laura wasn't the only person experiencing hell on earth.

You might notice that this book has a different tone than any of my other works if you've read them. Because life is so severe, I often employ humor in my writing, and I think laughter is something God appreciates. But if you look, you'll see this book lacks some of my characteristic humor. That's because, to be honest, when I wrote it, my mood was very different. I wanted to confront some of the more challenging questions we typically avoid asking ourselves about life's more significant problems.

I gave Laura the text to read after finishing the first draft. I said that I was doing it for her. She read the entire text in one sitting after bringing it home. She remained silent when she entered the office the following day.

Before we brought up the death of her child, a long time had passed. And it took even longer for me to share this manuscript with anyone. It was secretly stored in a hidden file on my computer for many years, mainly ignored. When I later learned horrible news about my daughter's health, I took out that manuscript and reread it myself. Unexpectedly, the words I had written for Laura were able to comfort me.

I decided to present the book to my publisher after some prayer. The depth of my passion was clear in words on the pages, and their editors felt that this message would resonate with others.

I then returned to the manuscript. I made some updates and additions. The outcome is this book.

Just to be clear, not everyone will enjoy this book. Stop and thank God for his benevolence if you're experiencing your spiritual high and living the dream. I join you in your joy. But honestly, this book isn't for you—at least not right now. This book is written with the hurting in mind. For those who have questions. For individuals who feel as though their faith is waning. For those whose outlook has become dim.

This book is for you if life seems to be creeping up on you and your faith seems strained to the breaking point. I hope you will have the fortitude to share in some of the sufferings of this planet with me when you read it. Again, you will notice the more somber and reflective tone, which I hope you can appreciate. This book explores some uncharted territory and battles some of the questions that Christians are often reluctant to pose. I pray that you come to understand the breadth and depth of God's grace that only the valleys of life can make known.

Although these words will touch many, this book is first for Laura, a close friend of mine. This book is also intended for the rest of us who suffer but don't know why.

Be Blessed,

Elijah

Introduction

The Meaning of Trusting God

Life is unpredictable and full of highs and lows. As a way to cope with life's challenges, many of us find comfort in our faith in God; at least, we hope to put our faith in God. During moments of joy and success, putting our trust in something greater than ourselves is easy. But we must persevere during the troubled and tumultuous times in life.

Even when everything around us is unstable, God remains a constant source of stability, security, and comfort. His unchanging and unconditional love gives us a strong foundation, even when our circumstances seem chaotic. Faith in God is not only an important part of our day-to-day lives, but it is essential to endure the hardships that life inevitably brings.

We place our faith in God, expecting him to provide us with certainty and security. In times of calm, when everything is going well, trusting God is often effortless. Yet when times are uncertain, it can be difficult not to panic. In these moments of instability, it is important to have faith that God is still there and always has our best interests at heart.

God's unchanging love and mercy provide us with a solid foundation to rely on amid difficult circumstances. He promises never to change and always to be there for us, no matter our circumstances. We can trust in his promises, no matter how turbulent the storms of life become. In times of distress, we can take comfort in his steadfastness and know he will bring peace and hope amid our trials.

Many of us take the precious gift of God's love and constancy for granted. We live in a constantly changing world, and focusing steadily on what matters most can be difficult—God's love. However, it is important to remember that despite the chaos and noise of everyday life, God's faithfulness never fades. His love never changes, and he will always be there for us no matter our circumstances.

God's faithfulness is a source of comfort and strength in the unpredictable journey of life. Whether we feel joy or sorrow, God's love will be our constant companion. Through good times and bad, we can rest assured that our loving God is with us every step of the way. We can find courage in his unending faithfulness as he provides a never-ending reminder that we are never alone and that he will never leave us.

God's faithful love speaks to the heart as nothing else can. When life feels uncertain, his unfailing love provides us with a secure anchor to cling to. God's faithfulness offers us hope and encouragement that, with him, even our most difficult moments can be conquered. By keeping our eyes on him, we can find the strength and assurance we need to keep going.

The gift of God's love and constancy will always stay with us throughout our lives. With his faithfulness beside us, we can confidently face every day, knowing he will never leave or forsake us. As we journey through life, let us focus on God's faithfulness, trusting he will always be there for us.

For a while, life may be moving steadily, without incident. Your work is fulfilling, and your family and friends are fun. Your plans, resources, health, and outlook all appear promising. Then, all of a sudden, life takes an unexpected turn. You know someone who gets sick. You lose your job. A close friend or relative betrays you. Things that you previously felt confident in now feel unsteady and unsure.

How can you stay confident in God's goodness in these conditions? Throughout life, our faith in God's goodness is often tested. When life events come crashing down upon us, it is easy to feel overwhelmed, like we are drowning in an ocean of circumstances and can't find our way out. This sense of overwhelm can cause us to question and even doubt God's goodness. We can't help but look for our solutions; when those don't work out, it can leave us feeling frustrated and helpless.

It's important to recognize the reality of these feelings and uncertainties, so we don't lose hope in times of difficulty. Instead, we must shift our focus to the bigger picture. This doesn't mean ignoring the present circumstances, but they should not be the sole source of our understanding. Scripture reminds us that our hope can only be found in God's goodness, even when this isn't evident in our natural surroundings.

The psalmist in Psalm 62:5-8 infers this same idea in his prayers of distress and discouragement. Even amongst his problems, he recognizes the truth; God is the only refuge, and the only place of security is found in his faithfulness. This does not mean we should expect immediate solutions. Quite the contrary, trusting in God's goodness may mean patiently walking through trials.

John 15:11 summates this truth beautifully: "These things I have spoken to you, that my joy may be in you, and that your joy may be full." This verse shows the overcoming power of God's love and should serve as our reminder that in the midst of life's storms, we can still experience joy and find confidence in God's goodness.

It is important to remember that God is in ultimate control, regardless of our lack of understanding of what is going on. He is faithful and knows our ultimate needs, sometimes far better than ourselves. The Bible says that in all our moments of despair, "God is our refuge and strength, a very present help in trouble" (Psalm 46:1). Our faith in him is what will sustain us. Only when we truly trust him will we find the strength to carry us through difficult times – and it is through faith that we will find that peace and understanding that come from his guidance.

When you don't understand what is going on, how can you trust God? No matter how overwhelmed we may feel, the Bible promises us a way out. Whether through Jesus' love, mercy, kindness, or strength, God will always provide us with a way to trust him through our doubts and fears. God does not keep silent in these trying times and has made a way for us to stay connected with him, even when a solution is not visible. There are times of prayer, Bible reading, and even worship that can be our source of guidance and assurance.

What do you do when a solution is not visible? Although it may not feel like it in difficult moments, God's ultimate goal is to protect and guide us in the right direction. We can continue to trust in his goodness and stay connected to him through all of life's difficulties. He will never leave us and has promised he will be with us every step of the way.

Trusting something or someone is faith in their dependability, honesty, competence, or strength. So, to trust God is to put your confidence in his dependability, his Word, his power, and his ability. The Bible asserts that God is truthful, constantly fulfills his commitments, cares for you, and has excellent plans for you. To trust him is to accept as true everything he says about himself, the world, and you.

Faithfully believing what God says, even when your feelings or circumstances lead you to believe otherwise, is what it is to trust Him. Your circumstances and feelings are essential and merit careful consideration. Both of them matter to God. However, relying solely on those things is not a solid foundation for living. They are subject to change at any time, even instantly. Contrarily, God remains constant. He deserves your faith because he is the same today as he was yesterday.

Trusting God is no cake walk. It can often be difficult, and it's easy to feel overwhelmed by circumstances and allow our emotions and realities to influence our beliefs. It's natural to feel discouraged when faced with adversity, and we all have moments of doubt and uncertainty. However, it's important to remember that trusting God doesn't mean denying those emotions or realities.

Sometimes, we may believe our emotions are so strong, and realities are so dire that it's impossible to fully trust God. This can cause us to act as if nothing is wrong or try to suppress our feelings. This isn't trusting God; it's trying to trust our abilities and resources instead. When we do this, we fall short of living a life of faith and obedience to God, despite our challenges and sorrows.

To develop authentic faith, we must journey through our feelings and realities instead. There is no other path to deepen trust in God. We must allow ourselves to come before God and express our true feelings honestly. We must be willing to move in the direction He's leading us, despite any pain and uncertainty that comes. This is what it means to trust God - even when it's complicated and difficult.

Ultimately, trusting God and following him is essential, no matter the situation. With a deepened faith and reliance on the Lord, we will experience true peace, hope, and joy - despite any challenges and sorrow we face. If we are brave enough to reveal our true emotions and realities before God and trust him despite our weaknesses and doubts, we will find the courage and strength to follow his lead and live life to the fullest.

Chapter 1
Life Won't Let Me Trust

Wiping tears from her darkened, bloodshot eyes, she said, "I want to think God cares about me; I honestly do." Under the harsh fluorescent lights of the hospital corridor, Velma bore little resemblance to the cheerful young person I had watched develop in our church's youth group. Velma was a different person in that hospital corridor than the one I knew from our church youth group who used to be so full of joy. Velma was a vibrant teenager who loved to worship and discuss God more than anyone.

Later, when Velma was in her early 20s, she met Stew, a wonderful Christian man with a charming demeanor. Nearly a year after they first met, they married after falling in love practically overnight. Stew's vibrant personality served him well, aiding him in obtaining a fantastic sales position, and he soon earned more than the majority of other professionals in his age group. As Stew and Velma served God together at our church after buying their dream house, they believed that life couldn't get any better.

They only tried for two months before discovering they were expecting their first kid. My wife, Melissa, and I went to the hospital with Stew and Velma to celebrate the lovely little Chloe's birth. We all praised God for this precious gift. It was wonderful to celebrate with them and give thanks for the wonderful family God was developing.

All of us were blind to any signs of cracks around the base of our lives back then. But as the years passed, Stew's job required him to travel more often and work ever-longer hours. But one day, Stew returned home and revealed to Velma that he was leaving her—for one of her closest friends—she never expected it! Devastated, Velma discovered that she had to fight on two fronts. On the one hand, she had to deal with Stew's betrayal, and on the other, she was struggling as a single mother trying to start over for herself and Chloe. Thoughts that at least things couldn't get worse gave her little comfort.

Chloe, who was then in the fifth grade, began dropping weight quickly and complaining of constant exhaustion. When the headaches and lightheadedness started, they sought medical advice. Several rounds of testing revealed the unthinkable—cancer. Chloe went from being a healthy, popular kid in school to a pale, immobile invalid on a ventilator in just a few short months. Cancer cruelly destroyed her fragile body, and chemotherapy barely made a dent. The doctors decided to focus on providing the most comfort during her final days.

The tenacious Velma I had previously known was long gone, gobbled up by this exhausted, despondent woman as I stood in that dark hospital hallway. She was severely discouraged, depressed, and exhausted. She frantically clung to anything that even vaguely resembled the limitless faith that had once come to her so freely. However, her unwavering faith in God was now little more than a painful memory. She took a deep breath and forced back the tears. It took all the determination I could manage to stay strong for her as her hopeless eyes pierced me.

She groaned. "I sincerely hope that God is with me at this very moment. I want to know that he is good and that he is concerned." She continued, "But Elijah, how can I submit to a God who can sit back and see my baby girl fading away in such agony, in addition to all else we've previously experienced? I wish I knew how to trust, but I don't."

I stopped at those words, "I WANT TO TRUST." Everywhere I turn, I see folks who can completely empathize with how Velma felt in that icy, clinical hospital. Many individuals desire to accept the existence and goodness of God, but they lack the necessary information. They have a deep-seated need to trust God—to know him, to experience his calm, to feel his presence among them, and to think that he will support them in bearing their responsibilities. They desire to pray and be heard by Him. They seek ease. They want assurance that he will defend them and be with them. Deep down, they hope God is more than just a fictitious cosmic character that foolish people blindly believe in. They want him to stand for more than the tired cliches that politicians, activists, and "Jesus freaks" like to use.

Many individuals like Velma used to think God was actively involved in their lives but are now simply unsure. *Does he care? Does he exist? If he exists, is he sovereign?* They don't feel Him. I have even been a part of that group (more about that later). You might belong to this camp too. Do you ever wonder, where was God when you were mistreated? Did he care? If he did, why did he not take action?

Every day, precious hearts ask honest questions. *Why can't we get pregnant? There are so many unwanted pregnancies; it seems like so many people have children they neglect or leave. We attend church faith-*

fully, and we are decent folks. We've been asking for years. Why won't God give us a child?

Why has my marriage failed? I wanted that to last, at least more than anything else. We used to love one another, and I certainly made my best effort. I believed him. Every day I prayed. But right now, all I have are fragments. Why did God allow me to experience this?

Why did my child have an impairment at birth? Why did I lose my job?

Why am I still single while everyone I know is married? Why do I feel like I can't advance? Why has the cancer returned? Why did my children turn away from the faith?

Do you want to be sure that wherever you find yourself, God will be there for you when you need him most, although doubt sometimes shrouds your mind?

It's not just you. People questioned God's presence in the Bible at various points. Even Jesus had to deal with skeptics, including the original Doubting Thomas, his disciple. But I want us to concentrate on Jesus' conversation with a spiritual skeptic. He was a parent who, like Velma, struggled as he saw his child go through hardship:

"And Jesus asked his father, 'How long has this been happening to him?' And he said, 'From childhood. And it has often cast him into fire and into water, to destroy him. But if you can do anything, have compassion on us and help us.' And Jesus said to him, 'If you can'! All things are possible for one who believes.' Immediately the father of the child cried out and said, 'I believe; help my unbelief!'" (Mark 9:21–24).

Can you imagine what that must have felt like for this father? He was helpless as his son writhed in the clutches of an evil demon that had possessed him for so long. This loving dad would do anything to take away his son's agony. Yet whatever he did, it was all in vain because his son kept suffering.

What must this man have experienced seeing his child thrown into fire or water with such ease by a powerful demonic force? But for this protective father, it may mean death for his son.

It is no wonder this weary and despairing dad couldn't grasp what Jesus was saying. When there were no other choices left for him to make, this man addressed Jesus in these words: "If You can do anything, then please have compassion on us and help us" (v. 22).

This question might invite criticism from some Christians however this father was at wits end and maybe he finally gave up after trying everything else.

He didn't know what to do anymore. There was nothing more he could do; hope had drained from him. He was living in darkness.

But then Jesus clarifies things by reiterating the father's helplessness as a question—If you can? —and then by posing a challenge: "Everything is possible for one who believes."

Just give it some thought. Why didn't Jesus offer his help by saying, "Well, I can help you"? If he were the Messiah and the Son of God, why wouldn't he have said, "My Father in heaven will heal your son"? These two statements were correct. Jesus, however, gave the initiative back to the father. Although seeking the aid of the one and only true and living God is always a good idea, Jesus claimed that the secret to success was believing and trusting that "with God all things are possible" (Matthew 19:26).

Even more startling is the father's reply: "I believe; help my unbelief!" (Mark 9:24).

Do you understand what he is saying?

He appears to be saying, "I want to believe in you, but it seems impossible. I have trouble doing so. Right now, I am stumbling. Please walk me through fear and skepticism."

The situation is somewhat paradoxical. This father, whose son has been held captive by an evil spirit and has tried to harm him in every way possible for many years, says that he would like to believe but no longer knows how. "I'm in such a desperate, hopeless state that it's difficult to imagine anything good happening. But still, I want to. If only I could. Oh God, give me faith again! Give me hope again!"

After this conversation between Jesus and the father, Jesus orders the spirit to leave, at which point the boy screams and looks to be dead. However, Jesus took hold of him and raised him to his feet, and after that, he stood (v. 27). The account affects me as follows: When Jesus expelled the evil spirit, the boy wasn't the only one who was healed. His dad had recovered as well because Jesus delivered him from the despair that had overtaken him. Jesus heard the contradicting messages coming from the man's battle-scarred heart in his direct appeal. And if we'll just let him, God still answers this request today.

Who are you? Would you want to have your heart, filled with doubt, healed? Wouldn't it be nice to reclaim solid, unwavering confidence in the person, goodness, strength, and presence of God? Even so, is that possible? Could God illuminate your gloomy, hopeless spirit with his light of hope? Could God sow a fresh seed of faith in the barren wasteland inside you?

You want to believe. It won't be simple to shed the old skin of doubt and skepticism, especially if the conclusion of your scenario doesn't match your aspirations and expectations.

Many of us still hoped that God would work a miracle for Velma's precious daughter, Chloe, despite the doctors' advice to her family to prepare for the worst. We then prayed. And we continued to pray. We used social media and saw what must have been thousands of people praying for God to heal tiny Chloe worldwide.

Sadly, God didn't act in the way that any of us had hoped. Just three days before turning eleven, Chloe passed away.

And in that instant, what little of Velma's weak faith was left broken apart into a thousand pieces. She yelled. She sobbed. She cried out, "Why, God? Why? Why would You allow my daughter to experience this? You ought to have killed me instead of her! How can I believe in a God who abuses me like this? How can I trust a God who would allow this to occur?"

I didn't claim to understand the reasons and didn't respond in a canned, pastoral way. Instead, I did what I could by praying alongside and for Velma. I joined the crowds of people trying to console her, weep with her, and support her.

I occasionally have pains, losses, and doubts like you probably do. But I'm still sure that God is with us in our struggles, and I want to work to help those whose faith in God has been destroyed by the wrecking ball of awful circumstances to rebuild it.

It's complex, and I only know some solutions. However, I have posed all of the same questions. I've learned something, and I hope it works out for you. You may battle with your faith and harbor doubts or questions. But you'll find something other, something much more significant. You'll find that these questions do not keep you from God's heart but draw you to Him. When you speak openly with him about your concerns, questions and deep pains, this conversation can draw your relationship closer than ever before.

For most of us, when we think about God, our relationship with him is distant. Nevertheless, being sincere with God can help shorten the distance between us and him while keeping the connection as well. In other words, we should not simply tell him what we believe he wants to hear but instead be honest with him and give him room to work in our hearts freely. This could be difficult because it requires sharing one's deepest fears, doubts, and pains with him, which may seem awkward and make one feel vulnerable.

However, if we take that step of faith and trust in him, there is so much to gain! By opening up to God and telling him what's on our minds, he helps us by comforting us more than any other person would. Even though trusting God at times like these is not so easy and being truthful may look challenging, he still is a loving God who perceives how we feel and compels us to find our worth and comfort in him.

In addition, being honest and truthful with God helps us recognize that he is an active part of our lives. It can offer us a newfound sense of clarity and purpose and show us that he is always looking to be a part of our story.

When we are open and honest with God, it creates a bond that is special and intimate. Our relationship with him can grow closer than ever, and we can experience the incredible blessing of having our divine Creator as an ally in our lives.

At different points in our lives, all of us ask ourselves tough spiritual questions, whether spoken or thought about subconsciously. I remember a sobering event where this man in our church, who had been happily married for 18 years, lost his wife. All was well, then suddenly, his wife was hit by a drunk driver. As I counseled him sometime after it happened, he suddenly said, "If there is a God, there is no way he is good! A good God wouldn't allow some idiot to kill my wife while allowing the moron to live! And if God is good, he cannot be in charge of events, or she would not have experienced what she did! Even the existence of God has lost its appeal to me. And if he does, I don't want to be associated with the kind of God who would allow such a thing."

His line of reasoning made sense. He raised several valid issues. And the reality is there is a real temptation for us to begin viewing God in that light when we are experiencing loss and rage. I'd even venture to argue that every time we experience grief, the enemy will attempt to use it to erect a wall between God and us. But faith isn't based on reason. Faith is a matter of the heart, not a subject of math, language, or even philosophy.

I haven't gone through the loss this man has. But my heart still aches for him. In addition, I could tell he wanted to put his trust in God below all his pain. He found it difficult to connect the suffering he was experiencing with the promises found in God's word. He was looking for a God-image to believe in.

I wrote this book for the many people who find it challenging to think that God is concerned about them, especially while they are going through a difficult time. Seeing the light when you're fumbling through a valley is challenging. You want to believe, but you need help to make the good news of Christ compatible with what you see in the world.

My family is currently going through a terrible experience, making this topic particularly personal to me. I am in great pain for my second daughter, Candace, just as the father we read about previously was in great pain for his son. Candace found out she had contagious mononucleosis, or mono, just two weeks before she married her college sweetheart, James. Her body never entirely healed from this somewhat common but unpleasant sickness, and even though she eventually conquered it, she now fights with serious physical problems that have confounded doctors. She was forced to cease working when she turned twenty-one—more doctors than I can count have seen us. And Candace is still in pain. She was devastated because she had to withdraw from college before the start of her senior year.

We recently booked airfare for Candace and her husband to visit the Mayo Clinic, hoping that medical professionals could identify the source of her physical difficulties. As I type these words, these are the questions I have right now for God:

Why her? God, she cherishes you. She always has. Why right before her nuptials?

How come you won't heal her?

Why aren't we able to at least receive a diagnosis?

We are not only inundated with honest inquiries, but we also regularly have been shaken in our faith. If you knew the specifics of her health challenges, you would understand why we often pray that she is not in danger of losing her life.

You can be assured that I'm writing to you from a position of both sadness and hope as I try to imagine the struggles you may be facing. However, there are moments when the optimism whispers while the anguish screams, and on occasion, it makes you wonder if God is even aware of your suffering, let alone cares and reacts.

If you're having trouble, you might be able to identify with Habakkuk, a minor prophet who is sometimes neglected. Habakkuk alludes to the same paradoxes and contradictory emotions that we saw when Jesus spoke with the father of the possessed kid and my friend Velma experienced after losing Chloe. The Hebrew word for embrace is Habakkuk, similar to the embrace that desires both.

The hope that God is still with you helps you cope with the pain of what you see and experience. The heart of Habakkuk is the kind that yearns to believe even as it shudders at the thought.

I'm hoping you're willing to wrestle if you're having trouble. So many individuals appear to be looking for a bumper-sticker God who makes life simple, trouble-free, and full of clever, even punchy solutions. However, life is never perfect. It's complex, and there are always issues. Because of this, it's foolish and even hazardous to think you can have God all figured out. To honestly know God, you must fight through suffering, contend with sincere uncertainties, and even live with unresolved issues.

A relationship with God is something that many people strive to achieve. After all, the presence of God exudes an aura of peace and contentment that few other things in life can provide. From mere acceptance of his grace to overflowing devotion and adoration, the level of intimacy between oneself and his or her God is something to be celebrated. However, through our struggles, we can realize how deeply we can know God.

Indeed, life is never easy, but we can truly know God in times of suffering. When we face death, heartache, or adversity, it is only through him that we can find strength and comfort. If we cling to God amidst the sorrow, we can ultimately receive glory instead of defeat. His hand is still extended and loving despite the harsh realities we face. We can recognize God's unending grace and ultimate goodness in such situations.

Examining our faith more closely can also be an effective way of furthering our knowledge of God. Sometimes our beliefs are tested as we must face skepticism and unanswered questions. Developing our faith despite our worries can allow us to mature emotionally and spiritually. Examining our questions head-on can challenge us in our faith, enhance our love for God and relationship with Him.

Furthermore, it is important to remember that certain issues will remain unresolved. Trying times can be difficult to understand without explanation, and the truth of the matter can be elusive. Nonetheless, it takes courage to keep searching for an answer and strength to trust. Even when our faith is tired and weak, recognizing God's underlying presence can sustain and uplift us in any situation.

To know God honestly and intimately, we must be willing to know that uncertainty is a part of our reality. Doing this makes it possible to realize the full potential of the beautiful relationship he can offer us.

Therefore, even though God does not guarantee that everything in our life will be perfect, we have this assurance from scripture: if you wrestle with God, seek him out, and cling to him, God will meet you in your suffering.

Chapter 2
God, Where are You?

The seeds of doubt can grow well in the presence of challenging experiences. However, one shouldn't wait for their life to fall apart to begin doubting God's existence and benevolence. My first experience with uncertainty didn't come at a challenging time; instead, it happened in a church, of all places, during an otherwise routine occasion.

My family and I occasionally attended church when I was a child. Naturally, when I was younger, I assumed that was how all families lived. In the same way that I believed that two plus two equals four and that the Dallas Cowboys were the best NFL team, I also assumed that everything I learned about God was right. But then, when I was maybe ten or eleven years old and sitting in church on a Sunday morning, a buzzing swarm of questions suddenly descended and started to sting my consciousness: "What if everything I've always believed isn't true? What if God doesn't exist? If he exists, does he play a role in our lives—in mine? Is he genuinely concerned?"

I turned to see if anyone else was having the same bothersome thoughts. Nobody else, or at least no adults, appeared restless or uneasy. (Later, I discovered that looks could be deceiving.) I don't recall what our preacher said, so it's not like I suddenly stopped believing what he was saying. But it was obvious that my youthful foundation of faith was beginning to fall apart.

The more I pondered these questions, the more I seemed to have. Why did so many awful things occur if God was in control (as he was said to be?) My life was wonderful; I had devoted parents, plenty to eat, and a warm, dry home. But I was old enough to understand that many individuals lacked those things. I had friends whose parents had experienced acrimonious divorces and friends who lived with only one parent. Children, I know, became so affected that they had to stop attending school. In a manner they had never done before, the news headlines started to alert me to the terrible things happening in the world daily: war, murder, poverty, and corruption.

Once those doubts surfaced, they persisted. They seemed to have found a way into my mind, and I wondered if I could ever get rid of them. Years of struggle with a personal spiritual conflict. Are you a Christian? If someone were to question me, "Sure," is how I would respond. At the time, almost everyone I knew would agree. We weren't Buddhists or Muslims, after all. I called myself a Christian, yet nothing in my life resembled Christ. Additionally, I was unsure about my true beliefs about God in private. I reasoned that my doubts would have hurt or disappointed him if he were real.

I didn't understand the gospel and what it meant to follow Jesus until college. There, I began reading the Bible for the first time in my life. I was astounded when I discovered that some biblical characters experienced similar questions as mine. Fortunately, many Bible parables and lessons answered many of the questions I had been silently pondering for years. It wasn't like I had just discovered a massive flyswatter that I could use to swat them all away at once. It was more like finding new routes through a well-known forest. Still, I could make out the trees and all the horrible things in the world, but now I could also make out the trail heading to the clearing in front of me. Although the trees were still all around me, they no longer hindered my progress.

Up until I went to seminary, where I accidentally hit a giant redwood.

"THIS IS MY OPINION OF THIS BOOK!" exclaimed my New Testament Professor as he hurled the Bible across the classroom in a sarcastic manner. "It's time you discovered the reality behind the fairy tale stories you've built your faith upon."

That may be difficult for you to accept, but it is exactly what happened. While I had some fantastic religious seminary instructors who helped me become a successful pastor, I also had those who were startlingly antagonistic; not only to the class in general, but to me directly.

I had been taught to believe in everything the Bible teaches about God, but my seminary experience was a rollercoaster of faith and doubt, hope and sorrow, just like life itself.

It was already significant enough that I went there.

As astonished as anyone, I was drawn into the ministry when I sensed God's calling. I wasn't hesitant; I just didn't fit the image I had in my brain of what a pastor should look like as a former wild frat boy, jock, and business major who became a Christian. In God's favor, my pastor asked me to join the staff to help the church reach some of the younger members lacking. My wife, Melissa, and I were overjoyed and grateful to be serving God in our church full-time.

I enrolled while working a full-time job when it became clear that earning a seminary degree would be a significant step in my development and essential for my future. Although all that added effort and study worried me, I was enthusiastic about the potential of bolstering my faith and improving my capacity to carry out everything I felt God was leading me to accomplish.

Imagine my surprise when I learned that several of my teachers and some of the other students had a jaded, pessimistic view. Only a foolish or uneducated person could genuinely believe in and accept the Bible as God's Word based on how they spoke.

The worst offender was, without a doubt, my New Testament professor. He would say that most of what we see in the Gospels is *NOT* what Jesus had said or done. This professor claimed that Paul only penned a small portion of the letters credited to him and that John wrote Revelation after taking some psychedelic drugs!

I was dumbfounded. Devastated. This guy had so many degrees and the entire alphabet after his name. In many theological circles, he was renowned for his brilliance. Someone with his credentials must be knowledgeable about the subject, right? The questions I had assumed were over and gone suddenly came back to life. Was what he said accurate? Was it conceivable that the Bible Wasn't God's infallible and inspired Word? Was there a God? But what if none of it were real? All of my earlier uncertainties resurfaced in my head. I had never told anyone when I was younger because I was terrified of what people might think. I was paralyzed by fear as an adult and a preacher. Nobody could find out. What might they say about me? Nothing is worse than a pastor who isn't sure of his beliefs.

So, I fought against my misgivings for a while, conscious of the several towering trees in my way. But eventually, I mustered up the guts to open up to my pastor and a different professor. These knowledgeable and responsible mentors encouraged me to wrestle rather than criticize me or dismiss my inquiries. They then helped in leading me back to the truth. The moments when they openly discussed their spiritual challenges and described how God had helped them overcome their uncertainties meant the most to me. My faith can be strengthened by honestly confronting my uncertainties, and God will prove his faithfulness in the process, as I learned from their real-life example.

Even though my faith was barely hanging on, it developed and became stronger. It seems as though God had carved a route through the doubts.

Until the mentioned obstruction in my path, I thought no one else examined everything they held dear. But in reality, we all regularly question our views. Your principles are at the forefront of every choice on how to react to someone being nasty to you. Every time you experience that physical soreness, a reminder of the urgent surgery you are still paying for two years later. You start to doubt your ability to heal, both physically and financially.

When your husband overdraws your checking account the same day your car breaks down, you must decide how to react and, more importantly, what will be the foundation for that reaction. When you scan the "headlines" in a news app about looming military action against yet another aggressive country, the most recent victim of a serial killer, or the number of fatalities in a train disaster, you are forced to consider your own beliefs—about human nature, about life, and God.

I'm increasingly convinced that doubts are necessary for our growth as believers as I've lived and strived to know and understand God. Let our doubts stand while we work through them rather than try to push them aside if we want greater faith.

According to what I perceive in Scripture, I'm persuaded that God rewards people who honestly seek the truth, much like that boy's Father who prayed to God for assistance in overcoming his disbelief because he so desperately wanted to believe (Mark 9:21–24). You may be able to relate, and you share the sentiment of many people who want to think but feel that life has gotten in the way.

More than a third of the Psalms consist of people's cries for help or songs of suffering. These inspired poems often express our suffering for us when we are unable to do so ourselves.

"Be gracious to me, O Lord, for I am languishing; heal me, O Lord, for my bones are troubled. My soul also is greatly troubled. But you, O Lord—how long? I am weary with my moaning; every night I flood my bed with tears; I drench my couch with my weeping. My eye wastes away because of grief; it grows weak because of all my foes" (Psalm 6:2-3, 6-7).

Do you understand David's suffering? He's worn out and worn down, depressed and lonesome. He has shed so many tears that he cannot shed anymore. He believes in God; it's not that he doesn't. He is a person after the heart of God (Acts 13:22). David doesn't understand why God, who can alter his circumstances and make him into a king of a nation from a mere shepherd boy, won't.

The authors of Job, Lamentations, Ecclesiastes, and Jeremiah all express the difficulty of tremendous sorrow faced by devoted believers and confusion, doubt, and pain. Even Jesus struggled to accept what he would have to endure on the cross and questioned his Father's decision in the garden of Gethsemane. Then, while he hung on the cross, he cried in agony, "My God, my God, why have you deserted me?" (Matthew 27:46).

God may occasionally allow us to doubt him in some odd way. He knows that's one of the ways our faith can develop.

I realize that's a contentious claim, and you might disagree. But it was my interpretation of the Bible that led me there. In addition to the ones I just cited, one more verse in the Bible allows us to question God if we're willing to listen to him in return.

Habakkuk posed many of the same questions that people worldwide do today, more than 2,600 years ago. And in his grace, God eased some of Habakkuk's suffering while leaving other issues unresolved. However, Habakkuk overcame his uncertainties to become a person with a richer faith. Had he not battled through his uncertainties, his faith would not have grown as fully.

Consider this. You wouldn't need faith if you had a complete and total understanding of everything, would you? But it is impossible to please God without faith (Heb. 11:6). Why? Because love is the foundation of faith and trust, not a corporate partnership, a financial transaction, or an unavoidable circumstance.

Are you prepared to wrestle with God with your many fears and doubts?

And perhaps more importantly, are you open to hearing God's response?

Chapter 3
Why Don't You Care?

Most of our thriller and crime movies are inspired by the Old Testament book of Habakkuk. Now, listen to me before you judge me as crazy. So-called antiheroes, or characters who misbehave despite noble intentions, are familiar if you've recently watched TV or movies.

When government or law enforcement corruption is depicted on television or in movies, we no longer find it shocking, and that now serves as a story cliche. Even when these antiheroes break the law to bring liars, cheaters, and murderers "to justice," we celebrate.

Why? We are tired of crooked, immoral, and unethical people getting away with their crimes, just like they are. We're tired of the "bad guys," whether they're drug dealers who pay off the police to avoid prosecution or business leaders who get seven-figure bonuses while cutting thousands of jobs from their organizations.

We could enjoy superheroes because they can fight villains who don't care about human life or follow the rules, which is why so many of them populate our neighborhood movie theaters. Thor, Iron Man, and Captain America appear to be doing things we sometimes wish God would do, but he doesn't. They don't go by the name "Avengers" by accident!

INJUSTICE. CORRUPTION. INDIFFERENCE.

These issues have existed virtually from the start of creation. Although not the first to do so, the prophet Habakkuk is undoubtedly among the earliest and most ardent. Habakkuk lived through a period of corruption, scandal, and brutality under the rule of King Jehoiakim that would have made the Godfather blush. Even among God's people, conflicts were often resolved through retaliation. While wealthy offenders poured coins in their palms, officials turned a blind eye. Poor individuals were often wrongly convicted of crimes committed by their rich rulers and punished as a result. In response, some started acting independently, like the heroes we root for on television and in movies. It was chaotic.

Only a little separated it from our society. Even if nothing in your life is going wrong and you're not experiencing injustice, what Habakkuk observed in the world around him still applies to us today.

How long, Lord, must I call for help, but you do not listen? Or cry out to you, "Violence!" but you do not save? Why do you make me look at injustice? Why do you tolerate wrongdoing? Destruction and violence are before me; there is strife, and conflict abounds. Therefore, the law is paralyzed, and justice never prevails. The wicked hem in the righteous so that justice is perverted (Habakkuk 1:2-4).

HOW LONG must I plead for help? I ADORE THE HONESTY IN HABAKKUK'S QUESTIONS. God, I have faith that you can intervene. How about you? Habakkuk calls God's attention to the fact that he tolerates the worst forms of violence and injustice despite being a just God.

What do you do when faced with injustice?

Imagine you are confident you deserve a promotion at work, but your supervisor promotes someone less skilled and less loyal to the company. It's unjust. You want to quit. But you need the money. You're helpless.

Alternately, you toiled assiduously on your last paper for a class. Your chances of getting into graduate school are dashed when it is returned with a C- when you are positive it deserves an A+.

Or you finally get the car you've always wanted, only to discover two days later that a careless, lazy parker has left an eight-inch scratch along the side.

Examples like these could irritate you, but they are merely realities you have come to accept. It's just a fact of life. That's just how things are in the world. Other things, though, are more difficult to understand. Things that are more unfair than you could have ever imagined. Things like Deception, Manipulation, and Betrayal.

Recently, I talked to a friend who had been a pastor for more than 20 years. After nearly 30 years of raising four children with his wife, he returned home one day to the shock of his life. His wife had decided that she no longer wanted their marriage. She had received a Facebook message from a former high school sweetheart. She had reestablished her relationship with the man, "God had planned for her to marry in the first place" due to a series of events.

The elders at my friend's church began conversing after she left. After such a controversy, they concurred that he wasn't qualified to serve as the church's leader. He had the choice to resign or be fired.

We wept together as this sad, battered man described his losses while sitting in my office. "God owes me nothing, but now I have nothing," he said. "How could he let me get divorced and lose my job after serving him my entire adult life? Where's the justice!?"

Where was the God he had spent so many years worshiping? Imagine someone embezzles money from your company and they get caught. However, instead of paying back the money they stole, they file for bankruptcy, and you will never receive the money back. Or how about this; what do you tell the wife of a good and hardworking man who dies of a heart attack at age 35 and makes her a widow? Particularly, consider how many haughty, cruel people you know who stay healthy and seem to outlive everyone else.

What if someone you've loved and trusted for a long time betrays you?

Everyone else considers her a strong Christian, which confounds you because you can't fathom how a decent person, much less a follower of Christ, could ever spread rumors about you based on what you disclosed to her as a prayer request.

You may have experienced injustice's sourness, firsthand. Even though you did everything you could to raise your children with love, gentle guidance, and the best you could offer, they still broke your heart. Even though you gave it your all, they are now drug addicts who steal money from your drawer to pay for their next addiction. All around you, young adults are graduating from college, landing excellent jobs, attending church, and getting married. The kids of your friends all appear content and prosperous.

You might have given your marriage everything, only to discover a betrayal that feels extra harsh because it was so unexpected. You believed you understood your partner, but now this? After everything you two have gone through together, someone at work had more to offer them? Seriously?

You're broken, crushed, and alone. No matter what the situation, it applies. We all feel the vicious punches of life sooner or later. When we receive a shin kick or a sucker punch to the chin, we're on the ground, and our spirits are left to bleed to death.

Yes, you do pray. You try to be merciful. You study the Bible. You rely on the sturdy backs of your Christian family and friends and pray more than usual. But nothing seems to be improving. The blows of life grow unrelenting, coming one after another. As a result of disappointment and unhappiness, your heart is battered and bruised, and your soul turns into a scarred and scabbed version of itself. You're gripped by sadness and numb with rage.

God's concerns and involvement in our lives is something many of us have puzzled over in our lifetimes. We often have questions such as, "Is God concerned about my fate?" We may even ask, "Why doesn't he intervene and change things in my favor?" The fact that God is all-knowing allows us to put our trust in Him.

We may sometimes ask, "Will he allow me to drown in all these negative things?" Some may feel that God is not interested in their lives and that they will just drown in their sorrows. This can be a valid emotion, but it doesn't need to be the final answer when considering how God views and handles difficult times.

God often uses difficult experiences to draw us closer to Him. The mistakes we may have made, and the consequences could have significantly affected our lives. However, even in those dark times, we can still learn valuable lessons; lessons on strength, courage, and faith. It may be hard to exemplify faith in difficult times, but it is essential to strong character and self-confidence.

Seeing an example of this in the Bible, Jesus was tempted many times in the wilderness, yet he never wavered in his faith, and that faith saw him through those hard times. Everyone can emulate that faith in their own lives, and having faith that God can and will intervene, even when all seems bleak, is one of the most important things you can do.

Therefore, rather than allow ourselves to assume that God will just allow us to drown without intervening, we can find truth and hope in understanding that God never gives up on us. No matter the circumstance or difficulty, God will bring us through if we have the faith to keep going.

God's timing is unique; his kindness and care for us are ever-present. We're encouraged to trust God, which often brings reassurance in uncertain times. No matter how helpless or overwhelmed we may feel, God can offer a positive outcome for difficult situations. All it takes is for us to ask for his help and to accept the strength he provides.

The power of faith is key to experiencing these miracles. By staying steadfast in the belief that prayer can work miracles, we can face our obstacles head on instead of being so quick to resist them. In certain cases, for instance, when we must decide on something difficult, it would be best to step back momentarily to seek advice and consider how God's hand may be leading the situation. The strength given by God can enable us to make wise decisions so that we will be able to enjoy fruits from living by his side even if we have to make hard choices.

Recognizing God's love and willingly working with it can result in miracles. Although we may get frustrated daily, trusting and relying on God will bring us peace and a brighter future. Even if that bright place is far away, God's strength will help us work towards it in a loving, peaceful, and kind way. With faith, we have the power to make a difference for ourselves and those around us.

The same kinds of inquiries we have were made by Habakkuk thousands of years ago. He reminds us that even powerful prophets who hear directly from God struggle with the questions of life.

Chapter 4
Habakkuk's Queries

The prophet Habakkuk was a man whose works of judgment remain to this day. He asked God many questions, which at first glance may seem strange, but these queries were integrally important.

Habakkuk lived in a turbulent time—the Babylonians had invaded Israel, and their wickedness was rampant. Habakkuk cried out to God and questioned him about why he wasn't doing anything to stop the wickedness and why he seemed to tolerate such injustices without punishing the wrong-doers. Upon reflection, it is clear that Habakkuk was looking for a sense of justice and wondering how God could allow such evil to persist.

While Habakkuk's questions may have been uncomfortable for some to grapple with, their importance lies in pushing people to confront the problem and take a closer look at God's justice and intentions. Habakkuk's questions challenged the long-standing conceptions of divine justice and allowed people to take a closer look at the moral complexities of their lives.

In addition to being a prophet, Habakkuk was also a poet. Many of his works remain to this day, and his examinations of divine justice, love, and power have stood the test of time. In his famous passage, "The Lord is my strength," Habakkuk stated his faith and trust in God, leading him to declare that despite all the injustice, God would protect and deliver the hand he chose.

Habakkuk's range of questions and reflections continue to provoke us today and can remind us of the necessity of remaining open-minded and continuing to probe God's justice. Throughout his lessons, Prophet Habakkuk challenges us to look at the problems in our lives—old and new—with a fresh perspective and continue asking difficult questions. In doing so, he reminds us that it is of the utmost importance that we never turn a blind eye to injustice and continue to strive for accountability and understanding with nothing but love in our hearts.

In Habakkuk 1:2, the prophet Habakkuk raises an important question to God – "How long, Lord, must I call for help, but you do not listen? Or cry out to you, 'Violence!' but you do not save?" As a follower of Jesus, I know this question is familiar to us all. We have all experienced turmoil, suffering, and despair in which it may seem God does not hear our cries for help.

However, God hears and answers every prayer, even if it does not seem like it at the moment. The writer of Habakkuk 1:5 reminds us that even when God may be silent, "The Lord is in his holy temple; let all the earth be silent before him." Even when it feels like God does not have a plan or does not care about our struggles, we can trust in the goodness and the sovereignty of our faithful and loving God.

In the same chapter, Habakkuk also warns us not to rely on our understanding but to trust in the Lord with all our might. Our faith is often tried and tested when we must wait on God's timing. We want instant answers and immediate solutions, but God may force us to wait or take a different path than originally envisioned. Rather than trusting in our ability to conquer any problem, the prophet reminds us to trust in God with all our might.

We must guard our hearts against doubt and trust in God's divine plan and purpose for our lives. No matter what struggles we may face in life, God is with us and hears our prayers. When we put our faith in the Lord and embrace patience through trials, we will be given the strength to persevere.

Habakkuk 1:3, he asks the Lord, "Why do you make me look at injustice? Why do you tolerate wrong?" When I ponder the question posed by the prophet Habakkuk of why we allow injustice to occur and why we tolerate wrongs in our society, my heart aches with sorrow. As a person of faith, I understand that our world is imperfect, and that God allows us to make our own decisions; these decisions often lead to circumstances that do not always reflect the justice we hope for.

However, that does not mean that we have to stand idly by while injustice and wrongdoing occur around us. Just as God has given us the ability to think and feel, he has also given us the capacity to act in a way that promotes justice and righteousness. As his children, it is our responsibility to fight against injustice and strive to right the wrongs that occur in society.

This fight begins in our lives as we strive to live our lives just and righteously. We can also become actively involved in our communities and within our local and national governments, engaging in conversations and activities that promote justice and work to decrease the occurrences of injustice in our societies. Through prayer, contemplation, and action, we can each make a difference in how we view and respond to injustice.

In Habakkuk 1:13, the prophet has more questions for the Lord. He writes, "Your eyes are too pure to look on evil; you cannot tolerate wrong. Why, then, do you tolerate the treacherous? Why are you silent while the wicked swallow up those more righteous than themselves?" First and foremost, it is important to remember that God has given us the opportunity to be his hands and feet in this world. We cannot be passive bystanders in the face of evil and wrongdoing, for God's eyes are too pure to look upon such things. We must speak out against the treacherous and to stand up for those who are treated unfairly.

When we stand up for what is right and fight against what is wrong, we live out the love for righteousness that God has placed within us. Our moral imperative is to fight against injustice and right the wrongs that occur in our society. The Bible never promises that injustice will ever be abolished on this side of eternity; however, as the church of Jesus Christ, through faith, courage, and perseverance, we can stand for righteousness to make a difference in this world as much as possible.

In a world that is all too often broken and chaotic, we can be a voice of hope and a reminder that there is still goodness in this world. We can use God's gifts to make a difference and effect lasting, positive change in our communities. We may not always have the answers, but we have the means to ask the right questions and work toward a better, more just society.

Focusing only on what is going wrong in our lives is easy. But we must not be so consumed that we miss the injustices happening to those God has placed in our lives. We must use our voices to call out injustice and challenge those looking to oppress or wrong others. Let us advocate for marginalized and vulnerable people and ensure that their rights are respected and upheld. Let us take part actively in our communities and do our part to ensure that wrongs are remedied, and evil is no longer tolerated.

God has blessed us with the ability to stand for truth and justice. Our eyes may be too pure to look upon evil, but there is still an active role that we can play in cutting it from our lives, our communities, and the world around us. Let us rise with courage and conviction and do all we can to bring everyone peace, joy, and well-being.

In Habakkuk 1:13, the prophet asks, "Why do you look on those who deal treacherously and hold your tongue when the wicked swallow those more righteous than they?" In our society, it is far too often that we see countless injustices being served upon those who don't deserve it. We look on as terrible events unfold but stay silent, and our tongues are withered and unable to speak up and condemn the wickedness presented in our world. We forget that God created us to be moral and just people, to help protect and defend the defenseless, no matter the cost.

It is not an easy task by any means, and it often feels like an uphill battle. The hate and prejudice we face can feel overwhelming, and speaking out can seem paralyzing. But in moments like these, we can reach back and draw upon our faith, empowered to fight for justice. To actively go out and take a stand for what is right, regardless of our fear.

We are here to help preserve and protect the good, eradicate the corruption of sin, and speak up in the face of injustice. To let our voices be heard and to let it be known that we will not stand for wickedness. We must remember that this is God's wish to raise our voices and speak his truth in every corner of the world.

We are a strong people, a moral people, and a people ready to speak up with conviction. This is who we are and the stand we must take. We have to speak up when others are being wronged. God will use us to be the moral compass the world desperately needs. We should never think we can't make a difference in the lives of others. We will always be people of justice, courage, and hope.

Chapter 5
WON'T YOU TAKE ACTION?

If life were more like a sitcom, all those antiheroes we talked about weren't as prevalent when I was growing up because there wasn't as much graphic brutality and corruption on TV. And it's probably for the best, as my parents wouldn't have let me watch those programs in the first place. My favorite classic comedies as a kid included Happy Days, The Brady Bunch, The Andy Griffith Show, and the scandalously racy Three's Company.

Despite being so predictable, the formulas were very satisfying. An unforeseen challenge faced by well-known characters led to plenty of one-liners and ridiculous slapstick situations. The Fonz, Sheriff Taylor, Alice, the housekeeper, Janet, Jack, or someone else, fixed the issue immediately before the credits rolled, and everything was back to normal in under thirty minutes—and even less than that when you account for commercial breaks! Even though I knew this wasn't how the real world worked, it was hard to fight the impulse to wish that reality followed a similar plot.

We all realize that the smooth, shiny surfaces of life on television have very little in common with the jagged edges of reality. It may begin early in life with fairy tales and Disney films, most of which have happy endings. But when a band of wolves with names like Cancer, Bankruptcy, or the Big Bad Wolves, like Divorce and Addiction, make the idea of a happily-ever-after difficult to grasp.

Who would have guessed that after being hit by a drunk driver and needing half a dozen spinal surgeries to walk again, you would develop a prescription drug addiction?

Who would have thought that when you partied a bit and had that abortion before becoming a Christian and subsequently fell in love with the man who would become your husband, you wouldn't be able to conceive?

Who knew that after pleading with God for a child and receiving one, you would lose your husband to cancer and raise your child alone while working three jobs?

Who would have thought that after only a few drinks—far fewer than anybody else at the party—you would be the one with a DUI that keeps getting in the way of your career? Usually, your life doesn't unfold as you imagine it would. The tricky part is that you can do any of those things when dealing with life's injustice, even when your mind is capable of coming up with various ingenious answers.

YOU WOULD KNOW HOW THE LAST EPISODE OF YOUR SITCOM LIFE SHOULD END IF YOU WERE GOD. After your operation is finished, you complete your first marathon. You are granted a full scholarship and are admitted to your top college. During the difficult time of infertility, you and your husband pray together and grow closer than ever, adopting a lovely young girl. You struggle to survive without your spouse until you meet that fantastic, single, attractive, godly billionaire in a small group at your church.

Naturally, you might not limit yourself to offering happily-ever-afters if you had the ability. Maybe you'd even punish all those selfish, arrogant, and cruel people who get away with murder (literally and figuratively).

Drug lords prey on the most defenseless, hooking them on an alluring poison that would eventually kill them. The bad guys who con older people and abuse children. The crooks in charge manipulate the system to exploit the underprivileged. Women are sexually assaulted by depraved souls who need to "feel like a man." Misguided women manipulate generous but equally misguided men to achieve their goals.

If you were God, perhaps you would ensure these evil people were thrown in jail! You would ensure they felt the same amount of suffering, loss, and harm they had wrought; they would endure no less than as much suffering as their victims.

God is perfect and all-knowing. Because we are not God, we don't always have the best judgment. The best choice that we can make is to put our trust in Him.

It is natural and understandable to trust in our own judgment. We feel that by being ourselves, we know what is best for our own lives and can make decisions to take us in the right direction. However, it is important to remember that we are imperfect and can miss the whole picture in life. We don't always know what is best for us.

God, by contrast, is omniscient and without flaws. This means that his judgment and plans are always best for us. We can have absolute confidence in him and his promises because he is perfect, unchangeable, and faithful. His plans for us are greater than anything we could ever imagine.

When we trust in God, we can have faith that he knows what he is doing and will guide us on the right path. Proverbs 3:5-6 says,

"Trust in the Lord with all your heart, and do not lean on your own understanding. In all your ways acknowledge him, and he will make straight your paths." When we trust God, he will lead us, give us peace, and direct us in all we do.

It can take courage and faith to trust in someone other than ourselves. But it is important to remember that while we may not always be able to see the whole picture, God always can. He alone knows what is best for our lives and will lead us on the perfect path. That is why it is so important to trust in God and rely on him for all things. He will never fail us.

When we ask God to do something, he often doesn't need to do much. A brief nod, a voiced word, or a response to prayer. A minor miracle in the grand scheme of things. If only he would let me be paid for all my effort! Or make my ill child well! It could aid in my relative's recovery from depression! Or stop me from abusing myself! Alternatively, return my prodigal child! Let me at least be the lottery winner!

We must be aware of what I believe to be some of the essentials of developing our Christian faith as we learn to trust God: Awe. Respect. Reverence. Gratitude for God's divinity. Acknowledgment of our human limitations. We cannot know every detail or peek into the souls of others. We cannot fully understand the course of world history and have no way of knowing how it will all turn out in the future. God can, though.

God is crafting an epic, like an expert storyteller. He has decided that each of us has an integral role—we are all leading characters. His story has no side characters or supporting actors, but all players are significant and inseparable. He isn't leaving anyone behind and is making every effort in our best interest.

God encourages us to be participants and writers in his story. He wants us to help create an intriguing, exciting, and momentous world filled with warmth, hope, and wonder. He gives us a chance to labor with him in creating his vision for the world.

With God in the author's seat, we can fashion a beautiful, inspiring story we can all believe in and take pride in being part of. To be collaborators in such an epic is a remarkable blessing, and to be chosen to have a role as it's written is an opportunity unheard of.

Therefore, we should remember that there is so much more going on than we can see or grasp from our limited viewpoint when we are suffering, shouting, and raving about all the unfairness of life. Only a tiny part of a much larger story—possibly only one sentence or paragraph on one page—is being shown to us.

"DEAR GOD, WHY DON'T YOU DO ANYTHING?" MAYBE THE QUESTION that gets to the root of our most profound skepticism. Essentially, we are pleading with God to bring our beliefs and what we see in front of us into harmony. It seems as though the natural rules we previously believed to be true quickly vanish.

When terrible things happen in this world and what we believe about God's power, goodness, love, and charity collide, we feel discombobulated. How can a benevolent God allow terrorists to fly planes into buildings? Or shooters to murder moviegoers in a theater or children in their schools? What kind of all-knowing God—I mean, come on—would allow infants to be born with leukemia, AIDS, and other severe illnesses?

How can our souls trust that God cares about us when our eyes see such heartbreaking scenes? This question can be a difficult one to answer. Today, we see great pain and suffering in every corner of our lives. With terrorism, hunger, poverty, natural disasters, and much more, resolving this problem of faith can be hard.

However, if we pay attention to God's word, we can see he did not promise us a perfect life or an absence of difficulties. Matthew 5:45 states, "For he makes his sun rise on the evil and on the good, and sends rain on the just and on the unjust." This brings us to the premise that God cares for everyone, good or bad, and takes away their pain and suffering.

The good news is that amid all this tragedy, God still gives us the strength and courage to move forward. He also guides us through moments of despair and instills hope in us. He ushers us closer to him in our moments of fear and grief and strengthens us. Our soul can trust that God loves us even in the darkest moments when it may feel like nothing else does.

Simply put, God never abandons us when hard times arise, and he even asks us to show mercy and love to those around us. His love for us never ceases, no matter how dark or unspeakable our pain is. When it may seem that no one cares, we can place our hope and trust in him and know he is always with us, comforting and supporting us on our journey.

God is aware of your suffering. Additionally, he invites your inquiries. He would prefer it if you yelled and screamed at him rather than walk away silently. You are welcome to express your deepest feelings to him, as David did in Psalm 56:8: You have kept count of my tossings; put my tears in your bottle. Are they not in your book?" Your pain, even your fury, is welcomed by God, but you don't have to stop there. Then listen after you've expressed your pain and concerns and after you've worn yourself out hammering on his chest.

He will communicate if you let him into the pain of your heart. Despite being all-powerful and omnipotent, God cares profoundly about you and rules over his domain. He will never leave you because he loves you. In reality, Jesus often comes to you at your lowest point, consoles you, and raises you to a place where recovery can start at last. But only if you're prepared to pay attention.

Chapter 6
It Seems Unfair

Sophie's Choice is undoubtedly among the saddest, most dismal movies I've ever watched. I wasn't old enough to see it when it first came out because I was still a child and had heard much about it by then. Meryl Streep received an Academy Award for portraying the Brooklyn-dwelling, Polish immigrant, Sophie.

Don't get me wrong, though; the acting, settings, costumes, soundtrack, and music score are all outstanding in this movie. But the tale is unbelievably tragic, and I should issue a spoiler alert and tell you what Sophie's actual decision is since I can't suggest it. We are made aware of the terrible truth that has plagued this woman through flashbacks of her torturous recollections.

Sophie and her little son and daughter learned to do whatever was necessary to survive while serving as prisoners of war at Auschwitz during World War II. The young mother was then given a horrific ultimatum by her brutal captors, who went above and beyond cruelty. She would have to decide between sending one of her kids to a work camp and sending the other to the gas chamber. Both children would be put to death if she didn't make a choice.

Sophie had to lose one child to save the other permanently. Years after she decided, the grief was finally too much for her to handle, and she ended her own life. It's both the best and worst movie I've ever watched. However, I was never able to forget it. I have six children, so I can't even begin to fathom what it would be like to pick one over the other.

IF YOU THINK ABOUT IT, JESUS DIDN'T HAVE IT EITHER IN LIFE. He was ideal in all respects. Jesus loved the unlovable. He healed the hurting. Looked after the rejected, Reached the inaccessible; Jesus could have argued the same thing we do if we saw his story from God's perspective: life isn't fair.

Jesus shouldn't have had to endure beatings, mockery, and floggings. It wasn't right that Roman guards cruelly hanged him from a device of torture and humiliation after driving stakes through his wrists and feet. They should not have spit on him, named him improperly, and chuckled as he had trouble breathing. The fact that Jesus—the spotless Lamb of God—became the offering for vile, filthy sinners like me was also unfair.

It can be hard to find comfort and reassurance when life is difficult. We all face moments when we feel helpless, embarrassed, discouraged, or overwhelmed; these experiences can be incredibly difficult to navigate. But I want to offer you some hope and perspective in an imperfect world. You might find comfort in the truth that God is compassionate and understanding; he knows that life can be unfair.

God loves us through all the difficult times and never abandons us in our distress. Regardless of the circumstances, God is always with us and ready to hear our prayer of lament. He isn't just aware of our tribulations; he empathizes with our struggles and meets us where we are. He invites us to turn to him when we are feeling hurt, angry, or confused because he knows that it is difficult to experience life's disappointments.

God has a practical approach to life's unfairness. He calls us to honor each other, even in our disagreements and speaks against the mistreatment of one another. He wants to see us make a difference in this broken world by expressing love, joy, and peace wherever possible. We can tap into his uniqueness and gain wisdom in navigating through the hurt by leaning on Him.

If we turn our attention to God when life is unfair, he offers comfort for our minds, hearts, and souls. He wants us to go to him in our deep sorrows and anguish. He is a comforting presence that brings understanding and clarity to our lives. He reminds us that hardships don't last forever and encourages us to remain focused on hope. We may not be able to immediately fix our challenges, but he teaches us how to bring light to a dark situation. God loves us and is eager to bring peace and comfort during difficult times.

Most of us probably don't give much thought to God the Father's agony and suffering at this loss, and I don't want to attribute God's feelings to those of humans. But given that God expresses love, jealousy, and compassion toward his people throughout Scripture and that we were made in his image, it is reasonable to conclude that God endured incredible suffering in sending his one and only Son to be born into our sin-tainted world.

But he could only establish a relationship with his earthly children in that way. He also allowed us to exist in a world that is negatively affected by our selfishness and sin by granting us the gift of free will, which, due to Adam and Eve, we wasted no time using. He tried the direct method, but his followers kept straying from him, searching for ways to obtain the idols, power, and lies that had driven Habakkuk insane.

Everything was out of order. The holy, just, righteous God was separated from his sinful, terrestrial, and imperfect creations. To remedy the problem, God built a bridge that enables us to know him, receive forgiveness for our sins, and be transformed into the likeness of Christ by offering Jesus—His own Son. However, God had to first let Jesus suffer in a way that must have felt painful to God as a Father, reminding me again of the agonizing *choice* Sophie had to make before giving up his Son (again, not fair).

However, God had to first let Jesus suffer in a way that must have felt painful to God as a Father, reminding me again of the agonizing *choice* Sophie had to make before giving up his Son (again, not fair).

One of my favorite writers, Philip Yancey, in his book, *Where Is God When It Hurts?* explains why God made such a sacrifice: "We feel pain as an outrage; Jesus did too, which is why he performed miracles of healing. In Gethsemane, he did not pray, 'Thank you for this opportunity to suffer,' but rather pled desperately for an escape. And yet he was willing to undergo suffering in service of a higher goal. In the end he left the hard questions ('if there be any other way . . .') to the will of the Father, and trusted that God could use even the outrage of his death for good" (Yancey, 2010).[1]

That lone figure on the cross, who declared that he could summon down angels at any time on a rescue mission but chose not to—because of us—was love condensed for all of history. God accepted his unbreakable standards of justice at Calvary. Any discussion of how sorrow and anguish fit God's plan eventually returns to the cross. "We must understand that the worst happens only once when people

---

1. Yancey, P. (2010). *Where is god when it hurts?* Zondervan.

wonder why good people experience horrible things. Jesus volunteered for it as well."

WE OFTEN FORGET THAT GOD IS COMPLETELY UNFAIR WHEN WE ARE BUSY COMPLAINING ABOUT HOW LIFE IS UNFAIR. You *did* read that correctly.

Not only is life unjust, but so is God in this particular instance. To be clear, he is never unjust by his standards but unfair by ours. We have good news in that regard. Since none of us would have a chance if he were just as we perceive him to be, we have sinned. We're naturally self-centered in quiet, understated, and blatant, dramatic ways. When we murder or commit adultery in our hearts, we are just as guilty in God's eyes as those who are caught and found guilty of the same crimes. Jesus at least said as much.

If we got what we merited, we would be abandoned and have no possibility for atonement, change, or an eternity in heaven. All there would be is the agony of remorse and the unbearable loneliness of realizing we received what we thought we wanted—to reject God's grace and be abandoned. To satisfy our egos, we would forfeit our souls.

Thank God, though, that is not who we are. Because God loves us so deeply, he never gives up on us. We are not animals; instead, we are people with everlasting souls even when we are injured, enraged, and angry with Him. Even when we are uncertain and distrust him. Even if we aren't sure of what we think about Him. Even when we doubt our ability to put our trust in Him. Even when we try to leave Him.

Indeed, in Habakkuk, we have someone posing the challenging questions; in this case, it's God's prophet. The Hebrew word Massa, which means "a dreadful statement, a doom, a load," describes Habakkuk's message. Habakkuk begins re-establishing a stronger faith, perhaps only by his willingness to name the elephant stomping around the room. What else does he employ? Not just a brief prayer over his meal but also a negative declaration, a weight. Sometimes the path leading back to God is not straight; it is covered with potholes and land mines. But God provides us with his Spirit to lead us, guide us, and lead us back to the security of his presence, nature, and goodness by guiding us through the maze of uncertainty.

What if, like Habakkuk, opening up and admitting your doubts is the first step toward developing a more robust faith? What if accepting your deepest questions paves the way for a developing understanding of God's nature?

What if experiencing genuine closeness with God means enduring something difficult to bear? To accept his power when you're weak from a burden, to trust him in the face of impending calamity, to hear him through a foreboding utterance? What if experiencing profound and enduring hope requires actual pain?

Chapter 7
A Crisis of Faith

Most of us have had summit experiences, which is often how many first encountered Christianity. We experienced God's presence during a beautiful event in an honest, palpable, all-encompassing way. We felt his love, grace, strength, and Spirit. We realized then that we wanted to devote the rest of our time on this planet and all of eternity to serving, pursuing, and making him known.

That is undoubtedly my story. I went alone to a quiet area near the baseball dugout at my institution after reading about God's grace in the second chapter of Ephesians. God's presence there was as palpable to me as the lunch I had just had in the cafeteria, but I could never fully express it. I sensed his affection and recognized his mercy. I heard him calling me to himself in a still, small voice. And that is when it took place. I knelt and begged him to take my entire life in my own words. I was a different person when I got up. That's when the spiritual metamorphosis got started!

No matter where I went, I had faith that God was there. I spoke openly about my faith with my fraternity brothers, teachers, teammates, and even adversaries. Every request seemed to be granted by the Almighty. I felt as though every Bible verse I read was written primarily for me! And it looked like God gave me the words to say and showed me a difference I could make wherever I went.

Being a Christian can at first seem like this incredible experience. You experience these potent periods of prayer and Bible study. The Bible's words appear to leap off the page daily, ministering to you just the right way. The sermons seem specifically tailored to you, addressing a significant issue you're facing or fully elucidating a verse you just read in the Bible. Then you recognize God is speaking to you when you see the same passage on someone's social media page. God played your favorite music just for you when it sounds on the radio as you get into your car. God continuously provides you with the right things to say as you feel compelled to help your non-Christian acquaintances. He is with you, you know. At the mall, a parking space becomes available in the first row while you're in a hurry.

Take a moment to imagine an enormous mountain. Upon the peak of a mountain lies a feeling of accomplishment that can be shared with few others. It is a sense of understanding and unparalleled satisfaction. Many have strived to ascend the mountain, and many struggle to reach the pinnacle. To summit a mountain requires dedication and a true sense of perseverance. Every step is a step closer to success, and the rewards that come along with the endeavor are truly priceless.

As you continue the climb, you must remember that although the journey is hard, it is worth the effort. Hardship, determination, and persistence are the attributes that allow you to keep pulling yourself up the mountain. The higher up the mountain you climb, the more you understand the importance of giving yourself the time to receive the stage and the process of making steps towards a goal. Glimpsing downwards and seeing what you have already achieved looks like a painting in the sky. You will know when you have reached the summit of the mountain as it is exhilarating and one that will bring a sense of accomplishment and pride.

If you commit yourself to the noble quest of reaching the top of a mountain, you will be rewarded with the understanding and feeling of success. By simply beginning the journey, you have already accomplished a great feat. Be proud of yourself and know that no matter what, you have the tools and strength to push through the tough barriers and will relish the moment of triumph when you reach the summit.

Standing atop a mountain can be an incredibly awe-inspiring experience. Gazing up at the beautiful vista of peaks and valleys in the grandeur of nature can often make us feel quite small in comparison. The realization of the vastness of our world, paired with the loftiness of a mountain, can put life into perspective. It gives us a chance to take a step back and appreciate the wonders of Mother Nature, explore the boundaries of our limitations, and look deep within ourselves.

With the humbling power of a mountain top, intertwined with the peace nature can provide, we often find an enlightening moment of inspiration. Regardless of what we are facing in life, a mountain top experience can be eye-opening and empowering. It can help us put a challenging life event into perspective and motivate us to keep going.

Sometimes, our problems can seem as large and formidable as a mountain in front of us. Even if progress may seem slow and the goals far off, faith in God can help us overcome any obstacle. Faith can motivate us to keep going, no matter what the struggle. It can give us the hope, strength, and courage to make it to the proverbial 'mountain top.' With faithful prayer and a steady spirit, no mountain is too high, nor is any river too wide. Nothing is too hard for God, and with his help, we can conquer any challenge that comes our way.

The incredible feeling of standing on top of a mountain is only magnified by faith in God. Combining the power of a mountain top moment with faith in God can make all the difference. It can inspire us to look far beyond today's struggles, making us believe anything is possible with faith.

The mountain-top experiences with God seem more frequent when we first become believers. We take for granted that they are the rule more than the exception. Then life circumstances gradually bring us down from the clouds, and God appears less present. Your faith no longer seems as remarkable now that you are back in the real world after descending the mountain without realizing it. You continue to attend church, try to study the Bible and pray whenever you have time because you still believe in God. However, the sermons seem like they only resonate with others. Your favorite song is no longer playing on the radio. And the prime parking spaces have all been claimed.

Life is suddenly not going as you had anticipated or intended. Your prayers seem trite and uninspired. It appears as though God has given up speaking. It's like someone duped you. God no longer appears to be as near as he once was. You're feeling lost and unsure where you stand with God or if you're still standing. You were on the mountain's peak but now in the valley.

I hope you never go there if you haven't already. However, I'm sure you're familiar with what I'm saying. One day you wake up and realize you're exhausted. You feel discouraged. Your faith tank is critically low, signaled by that tiny orange light that turns on. At this point, we reach "the dip." Author and marketing guru, Seth Godin, refers to the dip as the learning curve valley you must endure in your career while progressing from novice to master. Godin uses this image to make astute remarks about marketing and moving forward in your chosen sector (Godin, 2007).[1] I plan to use this image differently than Godin to illustrate the gloomy valley you must pass through after leaving the peak.

Something unexpected or even unimaginable is often the catalyst. The cumulative weight of multiple more minor yet complex occurrences may become so great that it causes a person's faith to crumble. In Matthew 11:30, Christ claims that his yoke is easy, and his burden is light. Getting out of bed in the morning doesn't feel very comforting. You're at a loss for how you'll get through the remainder of this morning, let alone a whole day. God has vanished.

Faith seems pointless at such a time. Shuffleboard on deck or a string quartet playing on the bandstand are difficult to enjoy when the Titanic is sinking. It's difficult to believe that praying, trusting, and hoping can help when you don't know whether the radiation and chemo will work, where the money will come from, or when you'll see your child again. When you have so little influence over the other aspects of your life, it might not be easy to keep the faith.

At times, the pain might be so severe that you can only think about getting some relief. Your entire being wants it to end. The pain is so agonizing you're more consumed with it than you are with Jesus. But this could prove to be a turning point on your spiritual journey. The fullness of God's grace is revealed to you in a way that is not conceivable when things are going well. He is truly present in your suffering. If you can understand that the route is through, not out, it can start to look more accurate in this valley than it was on the peak.

---

1. Godin, S. (2007). *The dip: A little book that teaches you when to quit (and when to stick)*. Penguin.

This understanding is a crucial aspect of the Christian faith: our convictions will be tested if we want to grow in our faith and get closer to Jesus. They should be examined. Blackaby & Blackaby (2009)[2] pose this question: "Will God ever ask you to do something you are not able to do? The answer is yes—all the time!" Some individuals may tell you that God won't give you more than you can manage. Even while they presumably mean well, that isn't the case. According to the Bible, God won't subject you to the temptation that is too great for you to handle (see 1 Corinthians 10:13). But he often offers you more than you can manage, which teaches you to rely on him entirely.

When you're injured, reading and processing those words can be challenging. Trust me, I am aware. Keep in mind: I have been there. And in my role as a pastor, I often visit individuals during their worst moments. It is never simple. However, God's faithfulness is constantly visible.

I once spoke with a man I'll call Stuart. As a new Christian, Stuart felt terrible for stealing money from his former job. After consulting with godly advisers, Stuart decided that confessing his wrongdoing and hoping for the best was the proper course of action. Unfortunately, the result was more on the opposing side.

Stuart's business filed accusations. Stuart was given a seven-year prison term even though he accepted his guilt and pledged to repay the money. Seven years for coming clean and doing the right thing.

Understandably, this situation would cause many to be furious with God. Stuart, however, claimed that his time in jail brought him closer to God than at any other time.

---

2. Blackaby, H. T., & Blackaby, M. (2009). *Experiencing the spirit: The power of Pentecost every day*. Multnomah.

A CRISIS OF FAITH 63

"His grace is enough, Stuart," was the signature on every letter Stuart sent me while he was incarcerated.

I was proud to hear of my daughter Candace's trust in Jesus when she was chosen to share her story with teenagers. A well-known international speaker from Australia asked Candace to speak at a sizable conference for women because she performed brilliantly. We could all feel that God was providing opportunities for our unique twenty-one-year-old disciple of Jesus. Then Candace became ill. The mono was already mentioned. But that was just the start. There were far too many complications that came next to list here. We were on the mountaintop together in a single instant. And the next moment, we fell into the valley on our backs in an avalanche.

Candace's faith does not appear to have faltered, but I have had some challenging discussions with God as a father. So, it's simple for me to patiently listen to those with severe religious issues. I used to not feel sympathy for them, but now I do. My approach to communicating with those who hold differing beliefs about the presence or goodness of God has also evolved through time. Years of maturing have taught me that it's not our responsibility to ram our opinions down people's throats until they agree. No, our task is to disprove their categorizations by acting in the same ways that Jesus did: by welcoming, loving, and forgiving them.

Because so many Christians try to act like they have it all figured out, I believe Christianity has suffered in recent years. This concerns the issue of suffering throughout the world. Let me reiterate that I have nothing against gaining a theological grasp of God's benevolence, alongside human suffering and wickedness.

Theology, or at least the capability or need to explain it, isn't always our priority when we're standing in front of a parent whose son has just been killed in a fatal shooting or a mother who has just discovered that her cancer has returned. When words fail, just being there and showing the love of God is more fruitful.

That is the incarnation's beauty and force. God didn't exclaim his love loudly from the sky. By taking on our humanity in the form of his Son, Jesus, he proved his love for us on this planet. Sometimes we might be better off listening to someone suffering than trying to explain what is going on. We put more emphasis on loving than on preaching. And in those times of stillness, God often makes himself known in ways beyond our comprehension capacity.

It's challenging to offer genuine compassion truly—and hope—to others until our suffering leads us closer to God. It's tempting to provide folks with facile responses and bumper sticker platitudes when we aren't linked to their suffering to protect our weak faith. Some individuals even tell those suffering that their pain is due to sin in their lives, a lack of confidence, or that they are simply receiving what they deserve. What a horrible, unbiblical, dangerously damaging reaction! I have never seen Jesus judge those in pain; instead, he used his grace to convict their hearts and make them aware of their need.

Our world is fallen. We shall all continue to meet excruciatingly painful, horrific, unanticipated tragedies in our lives because we live in a world where our free will has allowed our spiritual foe access. Not that becoming more mature in our faith exempts us from experiencing these things. The contrary may be more correct. We've endured enough suffering and become so much closer to God, even in our suffering, that our faith has grown stronger, deeper, and more mature for the next difficult period.

In his own words, author and scholar C. S. Lewis: "I'm not sure God wants us to be joyful, and he may desire us to love and be loved, I believe. However, we still behave like children, considering that the world is our nursery, and our toys will make us happy" (Lewis, 2001).[3] Suffering is the catalyst that must push us out of that nursery and into the lives of others.

Habakkuk knew this suffering very well. He fell into the valley and had a crisis of faith, and his observations and understanding of God were at odds. He found it difficult to understand why the God of Israel would do nothing and allow the kinds of horrors that.

Are you not from everlasting, O Lord my God, my Holy One? We shall not die. O Lord, you have ordained them as a judgment, and you, O Rock, have established them for reproof. You who are of purer eyes than to see evil and cannot look at wrong, why do you idly look at traitors and remain silent when the wicked swallows up the man more righteous than he? (Habakkuk 1:12–13).

Do you feel his suffering, his skepticism, his sense of unfairness? He essentially says, "Aren't you the eternal, all-knowing God? Why don't you act?" he reminds God that God selected the individuals currently punishing the innocent. Habakkuk states, "You can't even look at evil, but you allow it," in a tone that borders on sarcasm. Like many of us, Habakkuk is perplexed as to why God doesn't act following his expectations.

Remember that Habakkuk is a godly man! This is documented in the Bible, not some arrogant blog post from someone who despises Christians. Habakkuk was forthright.

We can ask God whatever question we want, and he can answer it. Although, he might not respond with a loud, audible voice. When we do inquire, he isn't upset with us. He won't leave the room if

---

3. Lewis, C. S. (2001). The problem of pain. Zondervan.

we have a temper tantrum. He understands. He wants to enlarge our relationship with himself even while we express our emotions.

He's given us the go-ahead to speak freely.

Sometimes I believe we are scared to ask God our questions, not because we fear his answer, but because we fear our own. Deep within the shadowy recesses of our souls, we are frightened to express how we truly feel. We're afraid our faith may crumble if we reveal our thoughts. However, the reverse is true. Our faith only breaks when we become so rigid and brittle that we shove down and reject the agony we are experiencing.

Perhaps this explains why some of us strive to avoid falling into the valley when we do.

We push our way back to the mountain's summit. We yearn for the intimacy we formerly shared with God. However, refusing to accept reality and rejecting things as they appear is like trying to climb a dune.

When her position is eliminated, a woman can reply, "It's okay that I lost my job. I am confident that God will find me a better job, and I'll wait for it to come to me while I sit here.

Or a man can reject the prognosis provided by his physician. "Nope. Not me. I'll continue to pray and have faith in God to heal me. There is no need for me to receive medical attention."

Please realize that I don't deny the possibility that God can (and does) heal individuals miraculously or offer jobs out of the blue. But we're not trusting him if we withdraw and turn away from him just because his answer does not meet our expectations. We are employing him and passing up better chances to improve. The peaks are lovely, but there are few farms up there. Why? Because valleys are excellent places for growth. Although your time in the valley may not be enjoyable, it is there that you develop a more extraordinary relationship with God and your faith.

C. S. Lewis and I believe our immediate satisfaction is not God's top priority. God is much more concerned about our hearts, spiritual development, and ultimate happiness. As a result, we must mature from a belief in a God who is incomparably wiser than we are to a more prosperous, ever-maturing faith. We must learn to follow him even when unsure of where he's leading us, trust him even when we can't feel him, and believe in him even when he doesn't make sense.

"Count it all joy, my brothers, when you meet trials of various kinds, for you know that the testing of your faith produces steadfastness. And let steadfastness have its full effect, that you may be perfect and complete, lacking in nothing" (James 1:2–4). Despite how contradictory that may seem, I don't believe James is advising us to give up and carry on. I think he is bringing to our attention the bigger picture, the bigger story, and the idea that something more important than the challenge we are currently facing is at play.

Habakkuk appears to have understood the significance of asking sincere questions while also having faith in God and his Word. Consider this: You can struggle with unresolved problems and still have absolute trust in God. God can manage it. And he loves you enough to be patient with you when you discover aspects of his personality that were previously too complex for you to understand your religious crisis.

This prophet was also ready to pay attention when God spoke, which, as we will soon see, he did. The good news is that God will provide for you when you most need him, and he will respond to you the same way he responded to Habakkuk. God has much to say about handling adversity, and he never declines our sincere questions to reiterate. But Jesus said, "Ask, and it will be given to you; seek, and you will find; knock, and it will be opened to you. For everyone who asks receives, and the one who seeks finds, and to the one who knocks it will be opened" (Matthew 7:7-8). So, feel free to ask whatever questions you like. Just be ready for God's response.

Chapter 8
LOST AND FOUND

My wife, Melissa, once asked if she could chat with me about the kids' plans for the rest of that week as I read through my sermon notes, checked my email, and replied to a friend's texts in my favorite chair at home.

"Sure," I replied. "OK, go ahead. I'm taking notes."

"Let's chat when you're done. It looks like you're busy," she said.

"No, it's OK," I said again. I was finishing a couple of things. After almost one minute, I still hadn't lifted my head to face her.

So, Melissa sat across from me and started uploading a week's worth of youth group meetings, piano lessons, soccer games, and dance recitals. And with six children, that's a lot!

I said, "Uh-huh," without turning to face her. "How can I help you?"

"You haven't heard a word I've said, Elijah," she admonished. She came across as somewhat frustrated rather than angry, which is quite natural when the person you're speaking to is preoccupied with something else.

I responded, "I heard you. You need me to take Matthew, and Celia needs to be at the church on Wednesday after school—"

She scoffed. "Oh, I'm sure you heard me, but you weren't paying attention." Ouch!

She was right. I heard but should have paid more attention. My ears perked up at the sound.

Her words were waves, but my overworked brain could not process their importance. Yes, we all tend to hear but not listen—multitasking appears to be the norm in our culture—but it doesn't absolve me of responsibility. Nowadays, most people pretend to be listening when someone tries to engage them as they watch TV, browse Instagram, text friends, answer emails, and update their calendars. Ask yourself this question: When was the last time you sat down and had a real, live conversation with someone else, taking turns and paying attention to what they had to say? No gadgets. No TV. No music. No other enticements.

Why is it so challenging for us to pay attention to God?

HABAKKUK BRAVELY ASKED GOD ALL THE HARD QUESTIONS THAT WERE ON his HEART, AS WE SAW IN CHAPTER 1.

He might have realized that sometimes all it takes to reestablish a relationship with God and develop trust in him is allowing yourself to ask these questions. If you're harboring resentments and hiding your emotions, loving anyone—even the universe's Creator is challenging. Despite his clear love for God, Habakkuk respectfully questioned God (as opposed to testing him; there is a difference) by asking for assistance in understanding the vast discrepancy between what he thought and what he observed all around him.

The prophet realized it was time to listen once he had finished his inquiries. We would benefit from doing the same. The prophet Habakkuk declared, "I will keep watch and station myself on the ramparts; I will seek to see what he says to me and what response I am to give to this complaint" (Habakkuk 2:1). *I'll keep an eye on my watch while waiting for God to speak to me.* As simple and straightforward as it may sound, there are occasions when our unwillingness to pause and wait for God to show himself to us is the reason we don't receive the answers to our questions.

Sometimes when we rant and rave, we want to let out our feelings without trying to talk to anyone. Our questions can overpower what God wants to speak to us if we let our rage, uncertainty, and fear rule us.

Other times, we may ask God a question, but because we're focused on the numerous things vying for our attention, we fail to pause and wait for his response. We hear but don't listen, just like in my one-sided talk with Melissa.

Why don't we take a moment to listen to God's quiet, consoling voice? I believe it's because so many of us are overburdened. We don't take the time to pause and quiet our hearts before God in silence because we're too busy managing jobs, home, school, and church obligations—not to mention whichever problem initially sparked our doubts—in our hectic schedules.

Psalm 46:10, God says, "Be still, and know that I am God." When was the last time you put everything on hold, sat motionless, and waited for God to speak?

God did not say, "Be active and know that I am God," as you may have noticed. He said to be still.

We know we must stay still and listen. But how does one genuinely hear from God? Many people want to have a closer relationship with God and ask how they can hear him. Recognizing God's voice amidst the noise of our everyday lives can be a challenge. Fortunately, there are various ways we can more readily tune-in to the voice of God.

Firstly, God speaks through his written Word. As we read his words, his spirit can bring to life whatever is read and teach us through the Scriptures. God often communicates to us through particular events in our lives. If we take the time to reflect on our circumstances, it is possible that God will offer us insight through them. King Solomon said, "In all your ways acknowledge him, and he will make straight your paths" (Proverbs 3:6). Additionally, wisdom can often come through other people. While it is important to never place anyone on a pedestal, considering whatever wisdom or life lessons they share with us is worth considering.

Finally, we can directly invite God to communicate with us. Through stillness, prayer, and silence, we can create a quiet atmosphere in which we can more easily distinguish God's voice from the others we hear. It can take some practice to truly recognize his voice. Still, once we give ourselves fully to him, we can cultivate the ability to discern his communication more effectively.

The key to truly hearing from God is spending time in his presence. In the act of stillness and quiet, we can open up to God's Spirit that transcends beyond the words we read in his Word to equip us with heavenly wisdom. As we listen, we can be sure our circumstances are not random; but are a part of his plan to reveal him to us and shape us for eternity. God is available and willing to have a relationship with you, and with the right approach, you can learn to readily decipher his voice. Engaging in things such as reading the Bible, reflecting on our circumstances, listening to others, and creating moments of stillness and silence will undoubtedly bring us closer to God. He is only a prayer away.

Consider it this way: One of the unanticipated advantages of going through a trying time is that it allows us to pause and reassess our priorities. We started spending more time with Candace and her husband when she first started battling her disease because of the difficulties it brought. We were motivated to spend more time intentionally with our other five children due to our time with them. Life's constant demands suddenly force us to deliberately slow down and embrace the ones we cherish the most. We often become more aware of what is most important to us when difficult things occur. Even if the talk with God would be challenging, spending time alone with him should be at the top of our priority list.

Habakkuk learned that when you ask God difficult questions, you must be willing to hear his answers, even if you disagree with them. Hopefully, if you seek God's presence while in pain, he will lead, direct, and comfort you. However, in the case of Habakkuk, God had different priorities. And it would be challenging to hear the news.

God commanded, "Look among the nations, and see; wonder and be astounded. For I am doing a work in your days that you would not believe if told. For behold, I am raising up the Chaldeans, that bitter and hasty nation, who march through the breadth of the earth, to seize dwellings not their own" (Habakkuk 1:5–6).

That is amazing. Shocking. And challenging to swallow. Is God empowering the adversary?

He basically said, "Here's the thing: you're right—my people have gone to a new low. I chose Habakkuk as my prophet and envoy to the Jewish people. Although it might seem like I'm letting things slide, I'm not. The Israelites are so wicked that I will have to exterminate them. And I'll do it with the help of the Babylonians."

I see Habakkuk's mouth opening in some profound, theologically sophisticated reaction like, "Say what?" God said that before things would get better, they would get worse. The constant conquest of various tribes and nations by the Babylonians earned them a reputation for being brutal, violent, and aggressive. Even while there was brutality and corruption among the Israelites, it was nothing compared to that of the Babylonians. It would be similar to asking God why he allows such injustice in our nation and then hearing him say that he would enable foreign terrorists to destroy us in response.

The last thing we want to hear when things are demanding is that they will likely worsen. However, we are aware that reality rarely follows our expectations. Then what?

REMEMBER THIS WHEN YOU'RE IN A SEASON OF STRUGGLING WITH GOD: The name Habakkuk means to embrace and to wrestle. You can argue with God about anything you don't like while accepting him because he is a decent and reliable person. What matters most is how we handle a crisis of belief. People typically choose between one of two extremes when they reach that valley.

Many people yearn to relive their most recent spiritual high when they felt the most at one with God. Their lives were going well, he was fulfilling their prayers, and their faith was strong. They tell themselves, "I'm going to pretend this crisis isn't happening right now," and dismiss all the doubts weakening their faith. Everything will be well if I ascend to that hilltop once more.

One of the guys I exercise with at the gym recently lost his job, and he never submitted any job applications since he was sure that God would provide him with another job out of nowhere.

By not filling out any applications or making any inquiries, he eventually had to move in with his friend and crash on his couch. He claimed that he didn't like manual labor and that he was sure God would give him a better job when I informed him about a lawn company that was hiring. I certainly don't criticize him for having such great faith in God's providence, but occasionally we need to leave the mountain and ask God to help us navigate the actual world.

Some people lose their footing and plunge even lower into the valley. "OK, God, if you're not going to do what I know you can do, then forget about you," they scream. I'm returning to the life I was accustomed to, and I wouldn't be able to trust you if you were capable of helping but weren't. They erroneously believe that if God doesn't do what they ask of him to end their pain, he must not love them.

Right in the middle of this second group is my friend, Vernon. Vernon discovered his mother dead in the bathtub in elementary school, and she tragically drowned while having a seizure. Upon discovering his mother's dead body, we can only understand the anguish a youngster would experience. How often did he cry himself to sleep, perhaps even accusing himself of neglecting to check on her? Anything I could do to get her back.

Vernon is older now than his mother was when she died, yet he still won't talk to God. Vernon said, "I want to believe that God loves me, but how can I believe in a God who would let that happen to my mom?" I'll never forget the pain I saw in his eyes. If there is a God and he allows such things, I don't want to be associated with him.

Fortunately, there is a third choice. We can start to climb out of the valley if, like Habakkuk, we're ready to lean into the difficulty we're going through and consider how God can use it to further his objectives. But you must remember that God is still at work even when things aren't going your way. From a human perspective, his interventions might appear enigmatic or even arbitrary. I'll use two examples from my own experience. In the first narrative, a prayer is answered miraculously, yet it isn't all that significant overall. The second concerns a much more significant personal prayer need and request. God could easily do it, but as of this writing, he hasn't.

First, Melissa misplaced her wedding band 23 years into our marriage. Because I was essentially broke when I proposed to her, the ring wasn't particularly pricey, but you can't place a value on the sentimental value it bears. Melissa was utterly devastated. She begged fervently that God would intervene for her to find it, and it didn't appear.

Eight months later, on a Sunday afternoon, we discussed the sermon I had just finished delivering at church. Everything centered on God's ability to heal. God can help you find what you didn't mean to lose, I had said throughout that message. Melissa then decided to recite the sermon's key phrase in her prayer. She told me she would do everything for God to point it out to us.

The most bizarre thing then occurred. I had this intense need to stand up. I moved past the sofa and the two chairs to the other side of the room, where there was a single chair. A shiny piece of jewelry was directly underneath the light-blue pillow when I raised it, and her missing ring was there!

I had never before seen Melissa dance in such a way.

You might laugh it off and say it was just a coincidence, but God revealed to me exactly where we could look for Melissa's missing ring.

God heard our prayers.

Now, this is where I start to lose my bearings. Melissa has had recurrent urinary tract infections for more than ten years. Because of how terrible these assaults are so often, she cannot perform everyday activities. She has tried every diet, vitamin, health drink, and supplement you can think of. She has undergone two surgeries and has seen the most outstanding physicians. There are countless times when we have prayed for healing. God hasn't healed her yet, though. Why does God want to help us in discovering a cheap, easily replaceable piece of jewelry but not to take away her constant pain? Why would he respond to a prayer that was so much less significant while ignoring our more urgent need for help?

You may be able to relate.

We continue to trust God even when we don't understand, listening to his voice and anticipating his response. And like Habakkuk, we will hold fast to God and put our faith in him even though he doesn't make sense.

Even if things might not get any better initially, the I-want-to-believer who will persevere in embracing God will become much closer to God than before. People closest to God often have experienced the most challenging circumstances, and God has proven faithful to them. Conversations with him—asking him and then calmly listening—forged their relationship.

Frank, one of my closest friends, is the most potent example of this I've ever encountered.

Frank first felt a ringing in his ear around two years ago, which continued to get louder until it became intolerable. After several visits to various medical professionals, Frank was identified as having tinnitus, a chronic condition. His condition is a 9.5 on a measurement of one to ten, with ten being the worst. Many people with less severe instances than Frank's commit themselves because they cannot handle the pain and noise. Sincerity dictates that my friend didn't want to live, but he was determined to end this never-ending nightmare.

Frank once took a plane to Atlanta to consult with one of the top tinnitus specialists in the country. This physician he met experienced the same problem as Frank. He handed Frank a specially made earphone that would make a competing noise to block out the continuous sound of a freight train in his brain. However, the doctor acknowledged that it probably wouldn't help much in Frank's exceptional instance. The finest thing Frank could do, according to this sage doctor, was to help others. You did read that correctly. Helping others can get you out of your own head and make you forget about your misery.

That is just what Frank did. Frank began doing more—way more—than just his regular amount of prayer and Bible reading. He and his wife formed a small group and started to nourish others spiritually. They began volunteering in various capacities within the church and "adopted" a single mother and her children to help them escape a dire predicament. Frank often complains to me that the buzzing in his mind is just as severe as it has always been, but it no longer bothers him as much. Frank occasionally tells me through tears that he is now closer to God than he has ever been. Frank is grateful for his terrible condition even though he would never choose this path or wish it on his worst enemy since it has allowed him to get to know God better.

Frank's tale reminded me of a passage from the New Testament where the apostle Paul talked about having "a thorn in my flesh" in his second epistle to the Corinthian church. Paul claimed he had prayed to God often to have it taken away. However, God didn't. As Paul puts it, the anguished prayer was this: "So to keep me from becoming conceited because of the surpassing greatness of the revelations, a thorn was given me in the flesh, a messenger of Satan to harass me, to keep me from becoming conceited. Three times I pleaded with the Lord about this, that it should leave me" (2 Corinthians 12:7-8).

Can you relate? *Heal, my loved one, please! He me in finding a better career! Please, Lord, help me to get accepted into my dream school. Save my dad, please! Get rid of my depression! Please get rid of my migraine headache attacks!*

But for Paul, the thorn persisted, and he eventually realized that God was allowing it to do more than remove it; God was using it to keep Paul humble and dependent on Him. God spoke to him, "My grace is sufficient for you."

His grace is enough because God is strong even in our weaknesses (See 2 Corinthians 12:9). It seems as though God was saying to Paul, "Look, I could remove this thorn for you. But if I did, you'd miss out on getting to know me better and fully understanding my grace."

Paul understood: "But he said to me, 'My grace is sufficient for you, for my power is made perfect in weakness.' Therefore, I will boast all the more gladly of my weaknesses, so that the power of Christ may rest upon me. For the sake of Christ, then, I am content with weaknesses, insults, hardships, persecutions, and calamities. For when I am weak, then I am strong" (2 Corinthians 12:9-10). Paul listened to God's response rather than merely hearing it. And just as it altered my friend, Frank, that slight distinction altered Paul inimitably.

It can also alter you. God's presence can help you even when you're at your lowest. Resistance in life improves faith in God, as resistance in the gym builds more substantial muscles. As you mature in God's grace, what formerly would have rocked your world gradually becomes something you can handle because you know he is by your side and will uphold you when you are weak.

That may be different from what you want to hear right now. If not, it's acceptable. I'm guessing Paul didn't want to receive this message. However, it served a higher purpose than Paul may have understood. As we know it now, the Christian faith might only exist with Paul and his influence. This suggests that the belief in Christ that's still evident in our society today may be partially due to this ordinary person refusing to accept that God had abandoned him.

It can be difficult to discern God's influence through us in our moments of hurt. In those moments, we feel so wounded that our confidence in God's faithfulness, protection, and care seems to evaporate. The value, purpose, and unique gifts he bestows upon us appear impossible to recognize. Our lofty ideals and religious convictions get distorted when we view the world through the scratched lens of a shattered heart.

Yet even in our pain, our darkened sight is not too dim or wrong to perceive God's love flooding our lives. We can look to the comfort of his presence, pour our grief into his Word, cling to the words of hope spoken by our spiritual mentors, and embrace the presence and strength of the Holy Spirit within. Even if our earthly understanding of the magnitude of God's grace fails us in our moments of pain, even when it is difficult to see – he stands ready to carry us.

God always extends his grace and mercy to each of us, no matter the circumstance. When we are discouraged, he invites us to reflect on how he has been with us in the past and how he is still waiting for us in moments of struggle. He is a compassionate and loving God with us and willing to take us as we are as we pour out our broken hearts before Him.

So don't be discouraged when it can be difficult to discern God's influence through you when you're hurt. For God loves you consistently, and he is present and will walk with you during this trial. He is a faithful Father who will not forsake you and will meet your needs with abundant grace, mercy, and comfort.

Perhaps you have been praying to God for what you require. That makes excellent sense; God desires our approach. But are you open to hearing what he says to you, even if his response doesn't match your expectations? Continue hearing. In your hour of need, God won't desert you; instead, he'll hold you close and help you get through the suffering.

Chapter 9
PUT IT IN WRITING

How do you respond when life hits you hard? What are your go-to strategies—the things you turn to for comfort? Since addictions are often constructed around the idols we turn to when times are tough, if it sounds like I'm questioning you about them, I probably am. It might be comfort food for some. For others, it can involve doing drugs, going out to parties, watching TV, or even passing the time on your phone, tablet, or computer. Your means of escape often make it worse.

A close friend discovered his marriage was having issues, and he turned to booze instead of seeking help from other Christians or God. And what initially dulled the ache started to impair his judgment slowly. He eventually acknowledged that he might need treatment after his second DUI.

For most of us, trying to ignore a situation or seek comfort elsewhere worsens things. We become even more frustrated as a result of the inaction. We might even feel bad for not being able to handle the thorn that has gone under our skin. In the end, we go even more away from the one and only one who can help us. Whether you're denying it, repeating Scripture, trying to return to your previous spiritual high point, or giving up your religion entirely, you're still avoiding the issue.

Until we're willing to engage in an open dialogue with God, that struggle

We will never feel the kind of peace that Jacob did, which hurt him and permanently altered his identity. But how can we do that?

Habakkuk provides three concrete clues. Habakkuk first questioned God's apparent injustice, as we just saw. He discovered that God intended to use the wicked Babylonians to destroy his people, so he paused and listened to God. Then, he wrote it down. "And the Lord answered me: 'Write the vision; make it plain on tablets, so he may run who reads it'" God instructed Habakkuk (2:2). And perhaps the toughest of all his decisions, Habakkuk understood that he had to wait for the Lord's timing and have faith in God to guide his people back to the mountaintop at the right time.

Not because I'm particularly old—at least not yet—but I forget something every time I go to the grocery store unless it's written down. Yes, I'm the one jogging back to aisle 12 for a bottle of ketchup from the checkout line. Even if it's just two or three things, I always forget what Melissa asked me to buy if I don't write it down or use the notepad application on my phone. Was it chocolate chip ice cream with almonds and cherries or chocolate ice cream with both? You wouldn't think it would matter, but it does. I now know I should put it in writing.

Habakkuk was making a public record when he transcribed his discussion with God, which included God's promise to save his people by first allowing them to be destroyed by the Babylonians.

Why would God want him to act in such a way? God made sure that his promises would be fulfilled for future generations—including ours—by recording them. God told Habakkuk, "Write it down so that everyone can remember that I am a God of my word when I prove myself just and true."

Remember what God says to you because your spiritual adversary is skilled at taking the truth seeds God intends to plant. You may have a notebook for these impressions or record them in your daily journal. God might reveal something to you, and if you don't capture it in writing or another method you can look back on, it's far too easy to forget what he revealed.

I can't even count how several times I've experienced this. I'll be praying and wrangling with something I don't understand. Are you there, God?

What is happening? What are you expecting me to do in this circumstance? What are you working on?

Then, I often feel God reveals something to me, guides me, or speaks directly to my soul. I've learned to put it in writing since, sooner or later, it will cross my mind again, and I will wish I had written it down exactly as it was revealed to me at that time. Without writing it down, my exact recollection of what God shared with me seems to fade.

But when I write it down, it turns into a spiritual anchor that keeps me connected to God and the reliability of his promises. "Yes, I think God has spoken," you say. "And even better than that, I have a benchmark I can refer to; it is independent of my state of mind or what I ate the night before."

You would be surprised at how much God does within the span of a year once you create the discipline of writing down what God reveals to you and what you're praying for. A well-known evangelist from the 1800s, George Müller, once saw hundreds of homeless children living on the streets of Bristol, England, and it broke his heart to see them.

Over the following sixty years, Mr. Müller aided in caring for more than ten thousand orphans despite having almost no money to his name when he decided to build an orphanage. He kept a journal of his prayers for the duration of his career, which ultimately totaled more than three thousand pages. He described a time when he prayed to God for help because there was nothing to feed the kids for breakfast the following morning. The next day, a neighborhood baker came to his home early. The baker replied, 'The previous night had been impossible for me to sleep, so I got up and cooked three batches of bread, which I had brought for them,' and Müller understood. In another instance, a milk truck happened to malfunction in front of the orphanage on the very day that no milk was available for the kids. The driver gave the milk to the orphans since it would have deteriorated in the heat (*God's faithfulness in providing*, 2016).[1] Mr. Müller is believed to have a record of thousands of specific answers to his prayers. Imagine how this strengthened his faith as he repeatedly witnessed God's faithfulness in plain sight.

If you're anything like me, keeping a journal can be difficult. I am trying to remember how I said I'd keep a daily journal several times, but by the middle of January, I'd forgotten and given up. Some years ago, I finally had a breakthrough. I was given a five-year journal, and I can't describe how much it has improved my spiritual life.

Keeping track of important events, prayer requests, and ideas in this journal is much simpler. Eventually, the pages will cover five years. For instance, five lines are available for writing on January 1 for the

---

1. God's faithfulness in providing. (2016, July 7). *GeorgeMuller.org*. https://www.georgemuller.org/devotional/category/biography/7

current year. Then, directly beneath those five lines are five other lines for January 1 of the following year, and so forth. In essence, you are only producing a quarter of a page daily. And you get to look back on what occurred yearly on that same day for five years. The highlight for me is? Getting started is simple because I have a few lines to fill in rather than pages.

I found it simple and meaningful the first year, and I could keep God in my thoughts while I recorded a prayer request each day, thanks to the daily discipline. But in year 2, I became aware of something that profoundly impacted me. I immediately noticed how many things that had bothered me back then were taken care of when I returned on the same day from the previous year to start the new one. Problems were resolved. Issues are resolved—answers to prayers. One of my children's issues had been resolved, and I was no longer even aware. It appeared like a significant setback when we lost a valuable employee, but a year later, we had someone in place who was even more productive. Our relationship has improved due to a friendship challenge, and we are now closer than ever.

I could see a more comprehensive picture thanks to daily journaling and a look back at the previous year, and I could see how faithful God was in ways I might have missed. I continued to focus on my current issues rather than looking back at earlier ones. And one specific discipline—writing it down—gave this realization its force.

Perhaps you're saying, "Come on, Elijah! I UNDERSTAND WHAT YOU ARE SAYING, but I'm not a good writer. Although I think it's a fantastic idea, do you want me to get on my laptop—or even crazier, take out paper and a pen—and write down what I believe God is saying to me?"

Yes, absolutely! You nailed it!

You should talk to God, pay attention to what he says, and write down what you think he's showing you if you're serious about getting out of this valley. Make the points you discuss with him concrete. The act of writing or typing words results in a testimonial that permanently records important memories and makes you a better steward of God's revelatory knowledge for you.

You may believe God is urging you to put your faith in him. Or to think he has something unique, perhaps even superior. Or you may feel that he is pushing you to solve the issue alone. You might think he is trying to change something about you through this experience. However, his postponement is not a denial. He wants you to learn patience. He wants to deepen your faith and instill patience in you. He wants you to keep hoping and asking, just like the persistent widow in Luke 18.

Could you put it in writing?

You'll develop your discernment by writing down what God is trying to tell you. Let me remind you of three critical ideas rather than go into an exhaustive lecture about how to know you're hearing from God. You might apply these straightforward recommendations to figure out whether the things you write down are from God.

First, remember that God communicates with every one of us in unique ways. Rarely do you hear a loud voice boom out of the sky; more often than not, you listen to the voice of his Holy Spirit speaking to you in the depths of your heart in the form of a whisper. God can also communicate with us through other people. He might impart his knowledge to you through your pastor, a parent, or a close friend. Additionally, God might use circumstances to direct, slow you down, or reroute you toward his plan. Of course, God also speaks to you through his written Word, convicting, directing, and encouraging you. But you must pause and pay attention. Turn off all outside noise.

Offset your phone. Go somewhere quiet and alone. As you listen, Again, to hear God, you must make time and space for listening to him. Write down anything he says when you do hear from him. Even reading this book, God might reveal something to you. If you have a notebook handy, jot down what he says in the margins.

Second, God often gives assurance. God gave me a vision for using technology to spread the gospel to more people in various regions years ago. Although I was pretty confident that this concept was from God, the fact that half of my church team had the same thought simultaneously served as a powerful confirmation for us all. God may communicate with you through other people, circumstances, a still small voice within, and by reading his Word. These will often overlap, depending on the message's focus. You have a thought that makes you question whether it came from God. The sermon that following week then addresses your notion specifically and uses Scripture to support it. Then, two buddies who aren't even close get in touch with you and each ask to discuss the same concept. Pay attention when that occurs.

Third, the communications we hear from God will always be consistent with his Word and reflect his character. You won't be asked to engage in sinful behavior or purposefully cause harm to others in the name of a loving and holy Father. Even though telling someone the truth might sometimes be painful, our job is to love them through it rather than condemn them. Our enemy will stoop to any level, often trying to distort God's message. However, the Lord is not a God of uncertainty; he can communicate with us if we are open to hearing what he has to say.

You can use it as a litmus test and anchor when you record what God speaks to you. Every time you refer to it, you can contrast it with what you see taking place in your immediate surroundings, which might aid you in making judgments. Be persistent and patient. As it did with our vision for our church, it can be years before what he tells you comes to pass. However, if God makes a promise to you, it will come true. It just depends on when.

Chapter 10
WAIT PATIENTLY

It's more complicated than ever to wait with 5G connectivity for our smartphones, access to the internet in nanoseconds, and same-day delivery from many large retailers. Nowadays, most of us don't have to wait around for very long. Just imagine how restless you become when your dentist runs late, and you must play three more games on your mobile device. Does it make you irrationally angry?

Habakkuk felt the same way about waiting. But he knew it was the third step he needed to take to emerge from the pit of despair. God told him that the revelation would come at the right moment and would not be proven wrong. Wait for it even though it seems to be taking its time because it will come eventually (Habakkuk 2:3). The Hebrew word for "assigned time" in this context is , which denotes the right moment, the set moment, and the divinely predetermined moment when God allows something to occur (Gesenius, 1979).[1] According to an old proverb, God is rarely early, never late, and always on time. Môw'êd sums it all together.

A pregnant mother carries the child for almost nine months before giving birth at the môw'êd. And trust me, nothing will stop that baby from arriving when the time comes; it will happen. I can attest to that. When Anna, our third child, was delivered, Melissa glanced at me while having contractions and said, "The baby's coming!" We were waiting for the doctor to arrive when Anna was born.

I said, "We should tell her to wait."

"The baby is coming now, I mean now!" my wife screamed.

Indeed, with no medical training, I had to deliver our daughter. As soon as her head appeared, I cradled it. Then, suddenly, I was diving low to grab her like a ground ball. As she was exiting, I would have patted myself on the back for being a hero, but I panicked and dropped her onto the bed. Even so, the drop was only a couple of inches. But I gave up because I couldn't handle the stress. It made me feel kind of good that I didn't faint. However, the other part—dropping my daughter—will never be forgotten.

I was powerless to stop her from coming until the doctor could arrive. When it's the môw'êd, neither you nor anybody else can make it go faster or slower. It will happen, and it will happen according to God's schedule.

---

1. Gesenius, W. F. (1979). *Gesenius's Hebrew and chaldee lexicon to the Old Testament scriptures, TR., with additions and corrections from the author's other works, by S.P. Tregelles* (S. P. Tregelles, Trans.) (7th ed.). Baker Pub Group.

YOU MAY HAVE TO WAIT A WHILE WHEN GOD PROMISES YOU SOMETHING IN his WORD OR OTHERWISE, BUT YOU CAN TAKE HIS PROMISES TO THE BANK. You may already be aware that you are in the waiting area. You questioned God about what was happening, listened to him, recorded what he replied to, and thought God revealed something to you. You're currently waiting, and you've been waiting, and you've been waiting. You may be beginning to worry that it won't happen.

You could have prayed for someone you love to accept Christ for eternal salvation. However, the more fervently you pray, the further away they seem to get from God. So, you hold off. You might be praying for a different kind of miracle from God, like for somebody to recover from an illness or to be liberated from addiction. Perhaps a disobedient child has crushed your heart. You've believed up until you're not sure you can believe anymore. You then continue to do what you have been doing: you wait.

When you feel your faith is about to run out, remember that whatever God has promised will come to pass. However, he will decide the timing, not you. If it helps, you're not the only one. Every believer must wait on God and expect his promises to be fulfilled as part of their maturation. An example throughout Scripture is an illustration of someone near to and selected by God yet still waiting. God made a promise to them, but they had to wait for it. Let's focus on a superior selection of them.

I will use you to deliver my people and restore the nation of Israel, God spoke to Moses. Moses then set out on a forty-year journey. Four decades! With the exodus from Egypt, a lot happened quickly, including the first Passover, plagues, running out the door, and walking into the center of the Red Sea before it dried up and submerged Pharaoh's army.

But the Israelites were expected to be eager to reach their new home after such a dramatic departure and nearly 400 years of enslavement in Egypt. They undoubtedly predicted that getting there would take some time. Several weeks, and maybe two or three months. Nonetheless, 40 years? It took that long, but God kept his word. To the promised land, he led them.

Why not consider Joseph? That guy with the rainbow coat, remember him? You're going to be a great leader over all your brothers and the whole country, God said to him. So what occurs? His brothers drop him into a pit, and we sell him as an enslaved person. Then Joseph is imprisoned after being unjustly implicated by his master's wife. Years passed until God finally fulfilled the prophecy and made him second in command over Egypt. That amount of time is excessive.

Here's one of my favorites right now. Paul the Apostle encounters Christ after having a vision. I'm called to preach, he declares after transforming. That is my purpose in being here. That's it. I must share the gospel. This is the only purpose in life that God has given me. Finally, he waits. Before that goal is achieved, thirteen years have passed. 13 years must pass before he can deliver his very first sermon!

Sometimes in life, you have to wait.

What are you going to do while you wait? Many compare it to getting stuck in traffic or standing in line at the supermarket. So, I'm stuck here, and I'll have to wait for this to pass. Nothing I can do will help.

However, there is a lot!

What is a waiter's job? They attend to clients who require food service. We ought to follow suit. We should always serve God while waiting, not just idly waiting for something to occur.

Waiting for him does not imply that nothing is happening. There might be more movement than ever as you wait.

The Bible commands us to "do everything in the name of the Lord Jesus, whether in word or deed" (Colossians 3:17), so, even when we don't understand.

We continue to serve God and carry out the necessary tasks as we wait to learn what God is up to and why we must walk through the valley we are in. I realize that's harder than it seems. What is a practical way to deal with insurmountable challenges?

Maintaining faith in God can be especially difficult when life throws us curveballs and we experience a mountain of hardships and unbearable feelings. Maintaining strong faith during times of adversity is essential to cultivate a trusting and positive relationship with our creator. Although times of hardship can be incredibly challenging, some strategies can help us keep faith in God and see the brighter side at the end of the tunnel.

The first piece of advice is to prioritize prayer and connection with God. When feeling overwhelmed and anxious, it can be tempting to hide from our Creator; however, reaching out and talking to God (or simply listening to Him) can be incredibly healing. Praying gives us space to Release our worries and heavy feelings while reconnecting us to the knowledge that God has our back and is with us through every moment. Secondly, it's helpful to practice reading the Bible or other books of inspiration to strengthen our relationship with God. Reading and understanding the inspiring stories of the Bible can help remind us of the Lord's sustaining love when times are hard.

In addition to prayer and studying scripture, action, and service can be powerful tools to build faith and bring light into our lives. Whether volunteering at a local shelter, helping our neighbor, or simply performing random acts of kindness, action can not only help us to take our minds away from our worries, but it can also prove God's love in tangible ways. Thirdly, we must remember to lean on friends, family, and our faith community for support when life is hard for us. Receiving and giving love to others brings hope and warmth, and it can be a powerful motivator to keep our faith in God alive.

Although keeping the faith during trying times is difficult, by reminding ourselves of God's love and the truth of his word, and taking action in the face of our hardships, we can gradually learn to trust that God has a greater plan and purpose, even if the path is full of bumps. Suppose we keep our relationship with the Lord alive and practice regular spiritual nourishment. In that case, we can keep faith in our Creator, even when the mountain of struggles we face seems impossible. Faith is an essential part of our relationship with God. In the next chapter, we'll look at the role faith plays in our daily lives.

Chapter 11
By Faith

There will be waiting when it comes to having faith. I love how God assures Habakkuk: "For still the vision awaits its appointed time; it hastens to the end—it will not lie. If it seems slow, wait for it; it will surely come; it will not delay" (Habakkuk 2:3). Knowing that God's timing is ideal is consoling. C. S. Lewis said it beautifully: "I am sure that God keeps no one waiting unless he sees that it's beneficial for him to wait." We may rely on God to act in our best interests appropriately (Lewis, 2009).[1]

When I was a child, six tiny words used to fill my heart with dread whenever I got into trouble—especially if it was something my mother found out I had done that I shouldn't have. She can emphasize a different word, such as "Wait till your *father* gets home!" or "*Wait* till your father gets home," depending on the seriousness of the crime.

My Father was a wonderful, devoted father. He never intended to harm me; he had my best interests in mind whenever he disciplined me. But like other children, I was constantly stopped in my tracks

---

1. Lewis, C. S. (2009). *Mere Christianity*. HarperCollins.

when I heard those terrible words. This meant it wasn't small enough that Mom would address it, but this error fell under the "Dad will have to tackle this" category. I'd be like, "Oh no. I should start praying right away!" When Dad returned home, he would discuss it."

After talking it over with Mom and me, he would take care of it. Any penalty or consequence was even worse than the anticipation!

I believe God told Habakkuk to wait in a voice reminiscent of my mother's. God said to his prophet, "I know you think the Babylonians are terrible and deserve some punishment. You needn't fear, Habakkuk; they will receive theirs. Just be patient. I am the Father in heaven. Because I am upright, they will pay for their transgressions." God appears to be pleading with Habakkuk to have faith in him and to take comfort in knowing that he will ensure that good triumphs over evil. However, it would take place sometime soon.

In addition to promising to punish the Babylonian people, God also makes it clear why they would suffer his wrath. These intruders from the adversary were haughty and exceedingly arrogant. We don't have to abide by God's regulations; we are more powerful than that. We have everything organized, and we've got everything under control. The Babylonians believed that they were God's unique case. The Israelites can follow such commandments, but we do as we like.

God then listed some of their significant transgressions. "Shall not all these take up their taunt against him, with scoffing and riddles for him, and say, 'Woe to him who heaps up what is not his own— for how long?— and loads himself with pledges!'" (Habakkuk 2:6). Then he scolds the dishonest people, saying, "Woe to him who gets evil gain for his house, to set his nest on high, to be safe from the reach of harm!" (2:9). He also paid attention to those who engaged in violence, saying, "Woe to him who builds a town with blood and founds a city on iniquity!" (2: 12). Finally, God even mentions the partygoers—yes, the partygoers. "Woe to him who makes his neighbors drink— you pour out your wrath and make them drunk, in order to gaze at their nakedness! You will have your fill of shame instead of glory. Drink, yourself, and show your uncircumcision! The cup in the Lord's right hand will come around to you," (2: 15-16)—and the idolaters in his litany of afflictions, "What profit is an idol when its maker has shaped it, a metal image, a teacher of lies? For its maker trusts in his own creation when he makes speechless idols! 19 Woe to him who says to a wooden thing, Awake; to a silent stone, Arise! Can this teach? Behold, it is overlaid with gold and silver, and there is no breath at all in it" (2:18–19).

Habakkuk's confidence must have been strengthened by God's naming of the Babylonians' transgressions and trespasses. God made it clear that he was fully aware of the situation, and he hadn't turned his gaze away and hadn't been distracted by anything else. When the môw'êd arrived, he had already chosen how to punish them.

Through a whisper, a person, or just by our faith-based assurance that he is with us, he shows that he is paying attention to us and our needs. He expects us to live by faith, relying on him and being of service to him while we are in the waiting period.

Our good friends Roger and Brenda recently told the rest of our small group about a recent trial. They are innocent, but a distant cousin is suing them, nevertheless. Brenda described how much God must want them to rely on him while sobbing. "We have done all we can," she declared. "All we can do right now is wait." She continued while wiping her tears away. "God teaches us to trust him by letting us endure this struggle because he desperately wants our love and attention."

I watched in astonishment as I witnessed their faith develop before my eyes, as a rose slowly opening its petals to bloom.

It should be noted that maturity of this kind takes time. It's a process that comes through spending time with God and is often the outcome of discovering how to trust him during a challenging situation. Although displaying this maturity in others is never simple, doing so helps us more than we may know. The book of Hebrews is the best place to look if you genuinely want to grow in your religion. The Faith Hall of Fame, a list of numerous people who fought, waited, lived by faith, and saw God's promises fulfilled, may be found in Hebrews chapter 11. People there are going through improbable — seemingly impossible — hardships but ultimately coming to a greater connection with God as they experience more of his power.

Noah saved his family by obeying God and creating an ark.

Despite being past childbearing age, Abraham and Celia were able to have the boy God had promised them through their faith.

Joseph endured incarceration, false charges, enslavement, and betrayal to preserve the people of Israel through faith.

God's people escaped Egypt by faith and crossed the Red Sea as it split on either side of them.

The Israelites marched around Jericho's walls by faith, and when they did so, the walls collapsed.

These were, by no means, flawless individuals. They all met difficulties and doubts, made errors, committed infidelities, and had defects and shortcomings, but they persisted in their faith and relied on God.

You'll get through this by having faith.

Consider this: you wouldn't need faith if you had all the answers and could survive on nothing but your knowledge. But not by religion but by your logic. However, it presents an extraordinary chance to strengthen your faith when something is unclear. According to

Oswald Chambers (1976),[2] "Some prayers are followed by silence because they are wrong, others because they are bigger than one can understand. It will be a wonderful moment for some of us when we stand before God and find that the prayers we clamored for in early days and imagined were never answered, have been answered in the most amazing way, and that God's silence has been the sign of the answer."

Veronica and Phillip are two of my favorites among the church staff members I often collaborate with. They prayed about adoption for a few years before deciding they wanted to pursue it. They consulted with placement specialists to help find a needy child, prepared a room in their house for a new child, and saved money to cover the expenditures.

They were happy to hear of a mother of two who was pregnant and had decided it would be best for her to give up her third child for adoption, even though they were open to adopting a kid of any age. This overworked mom was highly underprivileged, and she had struggled with drug addiction, and she now had to cope with as many "baby daddies" as she did kids. We rejoiced in our office over what appeared to be a fulfillment of our prayers for our friends.

After the baby was born, the birth mother had a change of heart. Veronica and Phillip were in shock. Their loss saddened them, but they were also worried that the conditions this lovely kid, whom they already loved, may be placed in would make her life much more difficult.

---

2. Chambers, O. (1976). *Daily thoughts for disciples*. Zondervan Publishing Company.

Therefore, this lovely pair acted as any other person would. They sobbed uncontrollably before crying once again. The following week, when I revisited them, I was astonished by their steadfastness in their faith. Veronica assured me after I had held them both that they knew God loved that baby far more than they did. They were putting their complete confidence and trust in God's omnipotent plan, even though they were undoubtedly disappointed.

This young pair was experiencing spiritual growth beyond their years. They were battling their dissatisfaction while yet accepting God's goodness.

You dig deep and remember your promises, trusting God by faith that everything is possible with him when your marriage breaks down, and everyone around you and your spouse keeps telling you that it's "simply too hard; you might as well get divorced." Even when others tell you that your children are hopeless because they keep making the wrong decisions, you have faith that God is working in their lives to bring about good for those who love him and are called by his purpose.

You must trust God to fulfill his promise to give you a child even if you can't conceive. He may decide to adopt a child for you rather than give you a child via birth. You continue to believe through faith despite anything he does. Even if you don't have enough money to cover the rest of the month's expenses, you trust that he will always provide for you.

You give ear. You record what God shows you on paper. Then, as you wait, you keep on having trust.

Faith is only faith if it becomes your only source of stability. Even when nothing is left for you to grab onto, you keep reaching for God. Even when things are not going well, you continue to move forward daily, one step at a time, to live by faith. You keep going. You don't give up, and you don't turn around. You go onward in faith.

Chapter 12
Faith Tested

What if, despite your best efforts, God does not fulfill his promise to you throughout your lifetime? Can you believe he will keep his word even if you don't see it while you're here on earth? Is it possible that you could become so close to God that you can continue to love and serve him amid your disappointment?

Because God did not fulfill his vow to chastise the Babylonians until the following generation, Habakkuk is a suitable instructor for us on this issue.

That amount of time is excessive. But the Lord remained dependable, and he is constantly.

When it seems God has broken his promise, Habakkuk gives us three simple words that we can hold to. Never lose these words, no matter what you are going through.

Here is what you hang onto tightly if you want to emerge from the valley and draw nearer to God. These are the three phrases you need to remember on your path to closeness and complete trust and faith in God if you want to be able to do so — no matter what. However, the LORD. These statements can be found in Habakkuk 2:20, where the prophet adds, "But the LORD is my strength; I will not fear."

After admitting that he still disapproves of the situation in his revered Temple. Let the entire world fall mute before him.

I will remember who God is, even when I'm upset, angry, confused, frustrated, dissatisfied, and impatient.

The Lord still has control, and he is also good.

He is a good man. He is real.

He is dependable.

He is all-powerful, all-knowing, and constantly present.

Despite how it may appear, the Lord is still present.

He is in charge and has a much bigger plan than I can now see.

He is God, and I must appreciate that I am not; my time differs from his.

His ways transcend everything I could ever understand.

He knows everything from beginning to end and is the wisest man in the world. I'm just a creature he created called a human.

Everything is in his hands.

OUR FAITH IS TESTED AT TIMES TO THE POINT WHERE IT SEEMS LIKE NOTHING IS LEFT. But now for the great news: Jesus said we could move mountains with even a mustard seed-sized amount of faith. Even when your strength is nearly gone, if you genuinely want to believe, you will push through with all your might to know and trust God.

What if merely wishing to believe is sufficient? What if that minuscule amount of inconspicuous faith is nonetheless acceptable to God?

What if the mustard seed of faith is the desire to believe?

In situations just as tricky and possibly even more intimate than those of Habakkuk, we encounter people who have been tested. The lives of Shadrach, Meshach, and Abednego were in danger. Although they had a hard choice to make, it turned out to be an easy one for them. They declared, "King Nebuchadnezzar commands us to prostrate and worship him rather than God, or he will cast us into this burning furnace. We won't honor a man, even if he's a prophet or king. We have faith that God will rescue us. We have faith that God will deliver us. But even if he doesn't, everything will be alright. No one else is receiving our submission but our Lord" (See Daniel 3:8-25).

Can you feel that strong, internal faith in a reliable God? They believed solely based on the kindness and character of God, not in the desired results.

These three young people stood up and said, "We know God can do anything."

"Shadrach, Meshach, and Abednego answered and said to the king, 'O Nebuchadnezzar, we have no need to answer you in this matter. If this be so, our God whom we serve is able to deliver us from the burning fiery furnace, and he will deliver us out of your hand, O king. But if not, be it known to you, O king, that we will not serve your gods or worship the golden image that you have set up'" (Daniel 3:16-18).

How could they be so sure of themselves? Why couldn't they accept a mulligan to save their lives and ask God for forgiveness later?

Considering that they had faith that God was in control, and that was sufficient for them.

They understood God was still God, even if they experienced a horrible, agonizing death in the king's furnace. They felt that the Lord was in control and that they needed to obey him.

What about Job, then? Talk about watching your entire life fall apart! Job lost everything, yet he was unable to understand why. Job's friends informed him that he was undoubtedly receiving punishment, but he could not recall anything he had done to offend God—certainly not to such an extreme. His wife counseled him to curse God and reject the one who had blatantly deserted him, and he declined. He instead acted on faith. And he deepened his relationship with God.

"Though he slay me, I will hope in him; yet I will argue my ways to his face" (Job 13:15). Job's confidence cannot be shaken by anything.

Your challenge may astound you by revealing a deep faith you did not know you possessed. These difficulties will demonstrate the sincerity of your faith, according to 1 Peter 1:7, "so that the tested genuineness of your faith—more precious than gold that perishes though it is tested by fire—may be found to result in praise and glory and honor at the revelation of Jesus Christ."

Even when God didn't provide Habakkuk with the expected response, he persisted in his faith. Although his life would get even harder, he remained faithful. He was aware that God remained God and understood that God remained in charge. Habakkuk repeatedly returned to those three simple words, "But the LORD," despite everything he had gone through.

Extreme situations call for solid faith. Do you understand that even a modest amount of trust is strong faith? This will encourage you.

Allow me to elaborate. A family from our church's twenty-one-year-old daughter experienced a severe seizure. She had intermittently experienced minor ones for years, but this one was different since she lost consciousness the entire time. Her family requested an ambulance out of panic. Unfortunately, when we learned the news, Melissa and I were abroad. Before we could eventually return and see this family, it took us a few more days. And the information got worse every day that went by. The physicians initially diagnosed her with brain damage. Then they explained that she couldn't survive without help because her brain was dead. Finally, they advised the family to discuss when to take their daughter off life support.

The entire family just burst into tears when we entered that room. We just sat there and embraced each other for hours as tears streamed freely from our eyes, and we were at a loss for words. The girl's mother then asked that we pray for their daughter. I had some ideas for my prayers, but I asked them how they would like me to pray instead out of deference for the sweetness and sensitivity of such a dire circumstance. The mother met my puffy eyes with her own; she wasn't exactly the most interested and devoted churchgoer. With a hint of resolve she remarked, "I know the experts say there is no chance, but I still want to believe that God could heal her."

A seed of faith was there. Not a lot. It was hardly a perceptible seed. But it was there.

We then prayed. And as much as we could, we hoped this girl would recover.

I often pray this kind of prayer as a pastor. I often officiate at that person's funeral a few days later. Things were different this time, and she soon started to get better. Soon after, she returned home. God had answered our plea, and he did the impossible. That family had the help of the Lord.

I also spent time with a different family whose daughter Bethany, age 19, had brain cancer. The surgeons felt reasonably confident they had removed every cancer cell throughout her two operations and estimated Bethany would live a long life. Tragically, she passed away unexpectedly nine months later. With a vengeance, the cancer had returned.

Some may wonder why God chose to be with the first family but not the second. I hope it is clear that God was present with them, albeit in different ways. God was with the first family as their healer and served as a soother for the second. They suffered one of life's most significant losses but witnessed one of God's most extraordinary acts of grace. He was by their side through every difficult day.

His mercy was sufficient.

God is still present even when you have nowhere else to turn, when your solutions and resources have failed, and when you have lost all power over a circumstance. God is still there even when your knees hurt from bending over to pray, but you're unsure if he's even listening. Even when people criticize you for having faith by laughing at you, God is still present. God is still present even when you don't know if you can live another day. God is still present even though the voice of your enemy is telling you to give up.

He cherishes you, supports you, and won't ever abandon or leave you. He will always be there for you. He might need to carry out your wishes more. But regardless of how strongly your circumstances would seem to suggest otherwise, he is always faithful.

Whatever occurs in your life, the Lord is present in his sacred Temple.

Chapter 13

Remember

"If you think God has forgotten you, then you have forgotten who God is." – Anonymous

I recently changed our bank account information over the phone. The customer service representative requested my account's PIN to confirm my identity, and I told her what I believed it to be, but it's clear that I got it wrong. When did I change it?

Then, in addition to my Social Security number's last four digits, she needed to know the names of my favorite childhood pets (which, in case you're wondering, weren't cats) and the addresses of two of our previous addresses. Thankfully, even if many of them were from ten, fifteen, or even twenty years ago, I could still recall all those things. I'm in awe of how incredible the human mind is, especially how it can store information in the form of memories. I recall conducting some research to explore the distinctions between short-term and long-term memory because this topic has always intrigued me. These two groups can be distinguished from one another primarily based on two traits.

The first is the importance we give to the memory we're recalling. The second is how often we think about it or how often we recognize that recollection or automatically think of it.

Crucial information like your Social Security number and the addresses of places you've lived for a while are permanently ingrained in your long-term memory. However, computer passwords and PINs, which often change daily for a few months, might be slicker. We merely keep track of them on the surface of our memories because our minds are continuously aware of the limited relevance of such things. Those kinds of specifics have a shelf life for the majority of us. Because of this, we rarely remember individual instances from our daily lives in the long term; instead, they must be exceptionally positive or negatively negative or stick out in some way.

Because of this, I can still clearly recall the fabulous steak supper Melissa made with love and care for our anniversary, but I can't recall what I had for dinner the night before. This explains why I can't recall what was mailed to me yesterday, yet I can remember what my children wrote on my last Father's Day card. This explains why I don't recall my most recent cold, but I do recall how difficult it was to get through a season when Melissa was seriously ill.

We often replay what is most important to us in our memories, which helps us remember it.

I SHARE MY LITTLE STROLL DOWN MEMORY LANE BECAUSE REMEMBERING WHAT GOD HAS DONE FOR US IS ONE OF THE BEST HELPERS TO CLIMB OUT OF THE VALLEY, not just for those mentioned in the Bible, for Israel as a whole, our friends or parents, or even our church, but also me.

Habakkuk recognized this. His prayer, described as "according to shigionoth," is found in his book's third and last chapter. Shigionoth is probably a literary or musical form, despite researchers being unsure of its exact meaning. The ESV reads as, "A prayer of Habakkuk the prophet, according to Shigionoth" while some translations say "on Shigionoth." In other words, Habakkuk chose a particular creative framework or environment to communicate his petition. The same person asking God some accusatory questions has changed his tune, even though we don't know the exact form. The Psalms show the same kind of progression—from skepticism to trust. It is comparable to singing a worship song that expresses how much we can rely on God despite how difficult life might be. It's another very significant step in the process of emerging from the valley.

However, getting out of the valley requires more than just seeming happy and going through the motions while you're hurting and tormented. When they are going through a financial crisis, their child's addiction, or the medical test findings, people occasionally tell me they can't attend church and sing joyful, uplifting praise songs. I reassure them that it's alright; we can all still worship God from wherever we are.

"O Lord, I have heard the report of you, and your work, O Lord, do I fear. In the midst of the years revive it; in the midst of the years make it known; in wrath remember mercy" (Habakkuk 3:2). He starts with this in a friendly, appreciative manner. It sounds like he is saying, "Well, God, if I'm being honest, I've experienced times when your presence seemed more tangible than it does now." When you were doing big things, and I am aware of the nature of the God you are. But kindly carry out identical actions once more for us. Recite all the wonderful deeds you've already accomplished. In this context, the

Hebrew word for "revive" is ḥāyâ, meaning renew, repeat, or restore (Gesenius, 1979).[1]

Following that, Habakkuk prays for several locations and occasions that are extremely real and obvious and will stir up spiritual memories in the minds of God's people. He names specific places: Teman, Midian, Mount Paran, and Cushan. The old mountains, rivers, streams, skies, earth, sun, and moon are among the other creations of God that he cites. We might respond to these verses differently than Habakkuk's audience did. However, the need to remember what God has done is timeless, even for us.

Habakkuk's prayer asks us to reflect on our key memories: those people, places, moments in time, and provisions that reveal the overall picture of God's presence in our lives. While it is true that we could research and appreciate the historical events that Habakkuk alludes to (and I recommend that you do so sometime), his prayer challenges us to remember our own. Habakkuk encourages us to remember God from the past rather than being so blind as to repeat our current, unpleasant circumstances.

The weird thing about memory is that. According to scientists, one of the most effective ways to remember prior events is through a process called "sense memory." Many studies have discovered that scent memories may be the strongest of all sense recollections. That is undoubtedly the case for me. When Melissa and I first met, she wore

---

1. Gesenius, W. F. (1979). *Gesenius's Hebrew and chaldee lexicon to the Old Testament scriptures, TR., with additions and corrections from the author's other works, by S.P. Tregelles* (S. P. Tregelles, Trans.) (7th ed.). Baker Pub Group.

this perfume, and now whenever I smell it, I think of our six children, if you get what I mean.

The delectable aroma of baking apple pie brings back memories of your grandma's house or a special meal your mother used to prepare. Similarly to this, music has the power to transport us back to a particular moment in time instantly. If you're my age, you probably remember your first junior prom or couples skate every time you hear Air Supply, Lionel Richie, or Chicago. (And if you're much younger than I am, you're undoubtedly curious about Lionel Richie, why someone would need an Air Supply, and what he was doing in Chicago.)

When Habakkuk speaks the names of these locations, the Israelites' memories of the events there immediately come to mind.

The Israelites sought shelter in these locations after God freed them from Egyptian servitude. The folks remember rushing out the door with nothing but the clothing on their backs, thinking freedom was no longer a pipe dream but a possibility. Suddenly, they can feel their hearts racing. They still remember the fragrance of the Red Sea and the sight of those enormous walls of water closing in on them after they had all successfully crossed. The Israelites all recall God's accomplishments, almost as if Habakkuk were saying, "Hey, people, remember when.

It's when we read a story to a youngster, make a ridiculous voice, or appear to yank a quarter out of their ear out of nowhere. How do they consistently react? "Do it once more, Daddy! Do it once more! I gave Melissa a children's picture book after we got engaged. She thought I was joking when I told her I was excited to read it to our children someday. And sure enough, six kids later, the pages are falling out of the book from how many times I've read it. The kids would ask me to "Reread it, Daddy!" night after night. Tell me also how you handed this to mom before I was born!

Our children adore this tale partly because they intuitively understand how it links them to their past, roots, families, and places of origin. Habakkuk recognized the significance of this remembering, and he helped the people remember by creating a clear picture of God, showing his glory and strength through nature.

He might have said, "God, I recall what you did," as an example. You astounded us all with your strength and glory. I recall the days you led your people by cloud and fire. I recall the time you fed us heavenly bread. I recall how the floods split; we could cross on dry land. I remember the moment you shook the ground and the walls collapsed. I recall when you defeated those who intended to harm us by sending downpours. I recall the times you unleashed famine and plagues against our adversaries. God, I'm reminded of your power. Now, kindly carry out those acts in the present.

AT TIMES WHEN I'M IN THE VALLEY, I NEED TO REMEMBER. Just think back on all God has done in my life, whether for me, through me, or even despite me. I go back to the God I know. I think back on what he has done in the past when I cannot perceive him in my current circumstance.

I recall being closer than you could imagine as a college student.

Imagine I yelled to Jesus, "If you're real, and if you're there, do something," almost daring him to respond. I will never forget that moment because what he did was so extraordinary. I met him there in prayer, went to my knees as one person, and when I got up, I was different. I cherish that instant.

I then think back to how God introduced Melissa into my life. I get to spend the rest of my life with my best friend, the mother of my six exceptional children, and my spiritual partner, which is still one of life's greatest miracles. I treasure her and the blessing that she has been and still is from God.

Then I go back to when our daughter Sasha was born and how much she loved Jesus as a little child. When Sasha was around three years old, I recall that she slipped into poison ivy and became utterly covered in a rash. She said, "Daddy, Jesus is going to heal me because I prayed," before she went to bed that night. Wow, that's pretty sweet, I thought to myself at first. But I was unsure of what to do if she still had that rash the next day. The following morning, Sasha ran into our room screaming, "Look! Look! he healed me!" while running around overjoyed that the rash was Gone completely. I'm in awe at how God responded to the child's plea.

When Melissa and I began in the ministry, we had no money, which was back when we were young. "God, we don't know where food will come from tomorrow," we prayed together. We received a refund check in the mail the next day. We thought God cared about us, knew what we were going through, and would provide. We still have that feeling.

I recall that when we first established the church, we had just relocated to a cafeteria in a primary school. One Sunday, I stood up in front of around 100 people and stated matter-of-factly, "The school said we couldn't meet here longer. Although I don't know where we're heading, God will provide. I also recall that someone allowed us to move into their facility on Thursday of the same week, a little bike factory. We began pulling down barriers and organizing the area because God had given it to us."

I recall erecting our first structure. And I remember when it began to fill up four times on the weekends, and we lacked the funds to start over. I can still clearly recall how it felt to turn people away due to a lack of space. I can still hear myself asking God to send us a miraculous present. Then a neighboring church contacted you and asked if they might join forces with you. After 30 days, their members decided to give it to us.

Join in what we were doing and take over their debt-free structure. I recall that day as amazing to me as Pentecost must have been for those early Christians.

I can still clearly recall going to see someone in the hospital. Her family came to say their final goodbyes and informed me, "They've stated she has less than an hour to live." While we prayed, I recall her vital signs changing at once. This woman returned home after two days, healed.

I still recall the time I was talking to a couple after church, and they sobbed as they admitted, "We've tried everything for seven years, but we can't have a baby. Can you say a prayer for us? "When I prayed, something that had never happened before and hasn't happened since happened. I recommended that they decorate their child's room after that prayer, though I couldn't explain why I would say that. And color it blue because God will give you a son in nine months. A boy was born to them nine months later.

You, too, recollect moments when God was tangibly present, regardless of where you are in your relationship with him. Your instances may not be as significant as the ones I just provided. Remember that it matters every time God moves or manifests himself. He consistently shows to us his presence and his concern for us. Perhaps it was when you were in excruciating pain and then switched on the radio to hear a song that seemed to be God's word to you at that precise moment. Or it might have been something as straightforward as reading the Bible and thinking, "Oh, my gosh! If ever there was a recipient for this verse, it must be me. Or when a friend called and said, Sorry if this seems unusual, but God put you on my heart, and I truly felt like I should contact you," when you were down and feeling alone.

When you're in the valley, what do you do?

You think about what God has done for you and how he comforted you while he led you. You think on when he gave you the exact answer to your prayer that you were hoping for, and when he deviated from your expectations, how in hindsight you understood that it was just what you needed. And then, you dare think he'll do what he's done once again.

Chapter 14
Accept

A few years ago, when our children were still pretty young, they went through their first crisis of belief. Even though I'm not a huge admirer, we've always had cats. Why? since my children adore them, and I also cherish my children more than I do pets. The kids loved our two cats at the time, Mittens and Muffin.

We once saw a bobcat running across our yard as we pulled into our driveway at night. The kids were delighted, acting like we had just seen Bigfoot; it was a bizarre experience. However, the tone of the bobcat sighting changed the following morning when Muffin did not appear for breakfast.

For the past five years, Muffin has consistently woken up meowing on the porch, ready to feed. I, therefore, couldn't help but wonder whether that bobcat had his little Muffin "muffin" for breakfast when she didn't show up that morning. After the second morning, the kids began to worry and ask inquiries, and I resisted the need to say anything. They then started to pray.

At the time, Sasha was three years old, and our boys were roughly five and seven. They all had such somber, depressed expressions, and they began cross-examining me. "Muffin is coming home, huh, dad?

Okay, Dad? Yes, we have been pleading with God for her to return. So, won't she return home? Because, you know, God wouldn't allow anything to happen to our pets!"

I didn't share my concern over Muffin's whereabouts, but I did say, "Well, I hope Muffin comes home." Like any good parent, I called the local animal shelters, posted lost cat signs around our area, and canvassed the neighborhood to see if anyone had seen Muffin. The children became more confident as we posted more characters, and they sensed that God would bring their cat back.

I had to invite them to a table and tell them, "Listen, guys. I'm sorry, but I don't believe Muffin is coming back." It was a delicate, sweet, and difficult moment.

And these tiny children, with their extraordinary, sincere faith, demanded an explanation. "But Dad, we prayed! Why didn't God bring home our cat?"

Therefore, I had to explain to them that God occasionally performs things beyond our comprehension. Perhaps even something that is painful lets us down or confounds us. And when that's what he decides, we must accept it.

Even though we are reminded of all God has done for us, things can still be challenging. Sometimes we have to move forward and acknowledge that something is beyond our current level of comprehension. However, we must also understand that acceptance does not negate the reality of what we are going through and how we feel. It just entails accepting the existence of the circumstance, expressing our emotions, and looking to God to see what he will do.

Denial is not acceptance. Even as you practice your smile in the mirror and commit verses from the Bible to memory, when you embrace what God is doing, you don't just shove your feelings down and let your heart die. When you acknowledge that God is working on something that you cannot see or understand at this time, you don't simply lay down and break or give up in despair. It would help if you continued pleading with him for a miracle until he instructs you otherwise, as he did with Habakkuk. But you don't act as though everything is fine when it isn't.

Unfortunately, I see struggling Christians trying to make their faith into something separate that they must put up with, like having to wear a wool coat two sizes too small in July. They try to appear cool and collected when there is no way for them to be. Because they have their heads in the sand, I refer to these believers as HITS Christians.

These people wear sand-colored glasses and abuse their beliefs. The doctor says your health could improve, and altering your behavior would help. They don't listen when I say, "We need to watch your heart." They buried their heads in the sand rather than confronting and embracing the truth. They say things when their marriage is in peril, and their partner says, "Look, we need counseling."

I understand what you're saying, but let's trust God for now; everything will work itself out. Their ears were in the sand.

When their funds are low, these folks will occasionally assert, "But I want the house. God has given me this house; I'm sure of it!" As a result, they take huge financial risks and incur debt that is far beyond their means. They buy the house "on faith," despite the advice of all of their trustworthy friends. They also buried their heads in the sand. Some Christians don't prepare for the inevitable fact that the storm will hit when it comes, and they avoid facing reality. They pretend we are all still in the Garden of Eden by sticking their heads in the sand.

Perhaps God is attempting to get your attention by sending you a message through your circumstances, such as, "Pull your head out—now!"

Habakkuk could not possibly continue to bury his head in the sand.

Habakkuk said, "I hear, and my body trembles; my lips quiver at the sound; rottenness enters into my bones; my legs tremble beneath me. Yet I will quietly wait for the day of trouble to come upon people who invade us" (Habakkuk 3:16).

He reacts viscerally. When something horrible is out of your control, do you ever get that sinking feeling in your stomach? You know how your muscles tense and stiffen, and you get headaches and stomachaches as your body tries to absorb whatever is happening to you? Imagine God telling you he intends to destroy you using the nation's biggest enemy. That was the situation Habakkuk was in. This will not be a fun season, he muttered, staring at the facts in the face. It's going to be terrible. Numerous innocent individuals will perish. Probably those I care about. Likely me. There will be a great deal of bloodshed. Even though I don't entirely understand it, I must trust God even when I don't like it.

It is not denying, and it is belief. Not the confidence that God will act in the manner that Habakkuk wants. However, trust in God's character. The sovereign hand of God is at work here, continues Habakkuk. Even though it may be challenging, I will embrace whatever God decides to do because he has spoken. You will experience something unpleasant at some point, which might be taking place now. Even if your cat doesn't come home, there are instances when you need more endurance, honest belief, and trust. How, then, do you climb out of the valley? If you study your desires and intentions, it can be hard to admit that God's sovereign will is at work. The truth of the matter is that even when we think God doesn't care about us, he always does things that are consistent with his own will. He wants what's best for you ultimately; his plans for your life are always good ones.

We may find a lot of peace in our hearts by reflecting on all God has done in our lives. It is advisable to know that "HE" had done this before we could get here. This journey has been full of faithful steps and decisions taken with love by Him.

When we agree to everything he does, it helps us foster more trust and faith in Him. His plans may be unfathomable, but obedience and trust are choices we make. Acceptance of God's will is an important aspect of spiritual growth that brings us closer to him. When we instill in our minds humility in submission toward his will, there is freedom in Christ Jesus as well as peace, which gives us confidence in his divine purposes.

Ultimately, belief in God's plans can help one accept his/her will. No matter how hazy tomorrow appears, however, we should remember one thing: God remains the creator who has a grip on every detail and whose purposes are always the best for his creation; ourselves included. We might not know what lies ahead, but let us take courage, knowing that he understands everything about tomorrow and that his plans for us lead to our ultimate good.

By embracing God's sovereignty over everything else again, tranquility and rest will return to our hearts. It's always helpful when we look back at what God has done us while keeping faith and trust in him.

Chapter 15
Trust

Even without trying to lead it, it was one of the most difficult funerals I've ever experienced. At age 46, Clark, a dear friend and steadfast member of our church, had passed away suddenly, leaving behind his wife and five children. Our entire neighborhood wept alongside them. I readily consented when his family requested me to give the eulogy at the funeral.

I didn't know where to start or what to say. Yes, I had a ton of sermons from past funerals and memorial services in a file, and many Scriptures, but none of it sounded right. Clark was a fantastic friend to our family. I was grieving alongside everyone else as I reflected on our interactions, the jokes he cracked, and the missions we went on together.

I stepped up to the stage to start the service but was still at a loss for words. I got going but then stopped. Paused. Flooded with feeling. Attempts to restart were unsuccessful. I suddenly had the impression that I knew exactly what Clark would want me to say to start his funeral. I took a big breath and, by faith, said what felt practically impossible in the face of losing someone like him.

"God is good," I said.

After a brief pause, during which it appeared as though everyone in the room was exhaling, they all echoed one another and said, "All the time!"

It was like a sigh of relief from the spirit. We acknowledged God's unfailing goodness even in the depths of pain and bewilderment. Some two decades later, people still bring up that event. It wasn't simple, but it showed our willingness to continue trusting God despite the intense sadness enveloping our hearts.

It takes trust to get out of the rut and use our crisis of belief as a launchpad to get to a higher, more personal plateau with God. We have to choose what we think is true, use our willpower to live out those ideas, and still be open and truthful about how we feel and how things seem to us. We often end up falling back into the valley if we let one of those components take precedence over the others.

Habakkuk provides us with an incredible example of how to react in a healthy, balanced way to what had to be the worst news God could have ever given him. He realized he could choose what to believe even as his body responded. He could rely on his feelings, and his perception of the circumstances was reliable. Or, he could have faith that God would use an unbelievable possibility—the invasion of their country by the Babylonians—for good.

"I hear, and my body trembles; my lips quiver at the sound; rottenness enters into my bones; my legs tremble beneath me. Yet I will quietly wait for the day of trouble to come upon people who invade us. Though the fig tree should not blossom, nor fruit be on the vines, the produce of the olive fail and the fields yield no food, the flock be cut off from the fold and there be no herd in the stalls, yet I will rejoice in the Lord; I will take joy in the God of my salvation" (Habakkuk 3:16–18).

Even though the news was so upsetting that he could not stand it, things weren't going how he wanted. Even though the problematic situation had just gotten worse than he could have imagined, he still decided to celebrate God's kindness. Habakkuk wept bitterly, much like all of us at Clark's funeral, but he could still declare, "God is good."

He decided to put his faith in God rather than any actual, audible, solid evidence he might come upon. "I'm going to delight in the Lord even though my body is a wreck, even though all the fruit trees and crops fail, even though we have no livestock" I mean, is that not crazy?

Years back, I was talking with a friend of mine who is a Christian counselor about the horrible, excruciating, and unexplainable things that people go through. He had heard me say that witnessing infants born with fatal flaws, kids who develop terminal illnesses, and young adults—talented, compassionate, God-loving teenagers—who pass away suddenly in a car accident, or shootings at schools are what I consider to be some of the biggest tragedies that make people question God's goodness. My friend and I agreed that those were some of the most difficult losses.

So, what do you say to folks when they visit you with that kind of severe, intolerable loss? I asked.

He gave me a long look before gently uttering the phrase "the truth." I awaited his following words.

He continued, "I inform them that I have no justification for doing this. However, God shares their sorrow and will use it as a catalyst for the greater good."

We remained motionless for a while after his statement.

"And you genuinely think that?" I asked. My friend couldn't have uttered those things unless he had suffered agonizing losses.

"Yes, I do," he replied. "It took me a long time—years."

He continued by talking about how a family friend had molested him as a child, his father's alcoholism, and his college attempts to avoid God through drugs, sex, and drinking.

He added, "We sometimes need to grieve the losses in our lives before we can make room inside for our faith to grow. The only way to do that when horrible things occur is to draw closer to God."

But what if the Babylonian invasion has already crushed everything you hold dear? You might still be mourning losses from a long time ago. But even in the midst of all that suffering, if you can decide to believe in God despite all the evidence to the contrary, you will reach a new level of intimacy with him. Even when you are hurting, you will be aware of his presence. When you don't fully understand your situation, you will be able to trust his character. Then, no matter what occurs or how severely your heart is wounded, you may keep moving forward for another day by taking one more step.

Your prayer, like Habakkuk's, becomes sincere about what you've lost or will lose, even as you acknowledge that God is still present.

I will still rejoice in the Lord, my God, even though my spouse broke their vow of "till death do us part."

Even if I taught my children to know better and they are currently making very unsettling decisions, I will still put my faith in the Lord, my God.

Even though we prayed for someone's health to improve, and they died anyway, I will continue to put my trust in the Lord, my God.

Even though we are in danger of our house going through foreclosure, I will still believe in the Lord, my God.

Even if my car needs $400 in repairs and my finances are tight, I will put my faith in the Lord, my God.

The Lord, our God, created us and has put us in a position of being his beloved children. So, when life gets hard, or we feel overwhelmed, or just down, our natural inclination is to pray to him and ask for his help. But sometimes, when the situation is dire, and the answers don't seem to come, faith in God can waver. I recently found myself in this very spot. I felt helpless and confused, questioning why God wasn't intervening more on my behalf. I felt he could and should be doing something more to help me, and this caused a shift in my faith.

But even though I didn't like it, didn't understand it, and felt God should be doing more, I chose to put my faith in Him. My faith wasn't based on feelings or what I could see, not on my power. Instead, I put my trust in God's promises, despite not understanding his plan or the timing.

This experience opened my eyes to faith's importance and trust in God's sovereignty. I realized that even in the most difficult times, he is with us internally and externally, never letting us suffer without purpose. I learned to trust his protection and guidance. I don't have to have answers or understand what's happening. Even though I still feel lost in moments, God is right there with me, taking care of me in ways I can't even begin to understand.

It is so easy to let the stresses of life and the feeling of being helpless to take control. But I'm thankful I chose to put my faith in the Lord, despite my doubts. I put my faith in God because he knows and understands me better than I can understand, and his perfect and infinite love will prevail. The Bible is full of God's promises. It keeps me going when life gets hard and all those feelings of doubt and confusion creep in.

When life seems too hard and impossible to understand, keep your faith in God and trust his plans. He is always there to salvage and turn our broken pieces into a beautiful masterpiece. So, even when I don't like or understand it and know God could and should be doing something more to help me, I will always put my faith in Him.

Chapter 16
Hope

The Shawshank Redemption tells the true story of an innocent man who was found guilty of killing his wife and given a life sentence in prison. It's a moving film with a strong message about freedom, joy, and hope. In a way, it's a modern classic.

But consider what it would be like to be in a situation where you were falsely accused of committing a crime you couldn't even fathom, much less carry out. Imagine being charged with the murder of six individuals, including four children! Consider that you would be executed for these crimes you did not commit. Imagine being informed of your upcoming execution date with a stay granted mere days beforehand. Imagine that you served eighteen years in prison before anything improves.

Anthony Graves experienced this terrible ordeal firsthand. After his case was examined by a law professor and her students with the Innocence Project, a group dedicated to reversing judicial injustice in our nation, he was ultimately cleared and released. Even the most tolerant, devout religious person would have been despaired by his experiences. His case was mismanaged at every stage, and the prosecutor in his trial was found to have engaged in "egregious misconduct" by the Texas attorney general.

Nevertheless, if you speak with Anthony today or listen to him talk about his experiences, you'll discover he's one of the most upbeat, motivating, and hopeful people you've ever met. His trustworthiness is unmatched. This man lost almost two decades of his life and reputation due to egregious injustice. But Anthony held onto his faith all that time. He indeed fought with God; once, after reading passages like the one in James 1 that tells us to count it all joy when we go through tribulations, he threw his Bible at the wall in his cell (Graves, 2018).[1]

But he soon saw the reality of his predicament. He wasn't guilty. Anthony was more confident every day that God had not deserted him and would somehow bring something good—something he could not possibly understand on his own—out of this horrific experience. He and God were the only ones who knew this and the actual killer.

To Anthony Graves, God kept his promise. Anthony discusses criminal justice reform, the death penalty, and prison reform in his speeches, blogs, and writings. Now, tens of thousands of people are affected by his narrative. His love for God and belief in Jesus are pretty straightforward, and he understands what it is to be hopeful in the face of overwhelming odds. You may experience the same thing.

HABAKKUK WAS NOT IMPRISONED, BUT HE KNEW WHAT IT WAS LIKE TO FEEL CONSTRICTED BY DESPICABLE CONDITIONS. As we've seen, he was still able to reflect on everything that God had done for him, to acknowledge that God was

---

1. Graves, A. (2018). *Infinite hope: How wrongful conviction, solitary confinement, and 12 years on death row failed to kill my soul*. Beacon Press.

working behind the scenes and in ways that aren't immediately apparent, and to have faith that God would raise something magnificent from the ashes of the here and now. "God, the Lord, is my strength; he makes my feet like the deer's; he makes me tread on my high places (Habakkuk 3:19a).

It is impressive that he can recite this prayer when you consider what this prophet knew he was already facing and that it was about to worsen when the Babylonians arrived in town. "The Lord is in his holy temple, even though the fig tree doesn't bud and there aren't any animals in the barn. Be still, all the earth before him, even though things will worsen before they get better. By faith, the godly will live. God's word is trustworthy. The Lord, my God, is where I shall find strength and hope; he will help me reach new heights."

It reminds me of my friend Turner, a man I met through a high school job. Unfortunately, Turner's bad, immoral choices forced him into a corner.

Turner's wife had enough after finding out that he had cheated on her twice. Turner regrets his sins now that she has left him and can quickly see how he strayed from the straight and narrow path. He is actively pursuing the Lord now, but his life is still in disarray. There is currently no sign that his life will ever get better how we all hope it will. He isn't giving up, though. I always tell him that God is with him when we communicate. And every day, the power of God sustains him and helps him endure the suffering of his present state. His marriage has not yet been saved, and his children are still upset. He also hasn't discovered a new life goal. But I am confident that God will continue to uphold Turner daily and deliver a new narrative of repair that will materialize over time. Because the Lord rules over him, and he is consistently dependable.

Habakkuk contrasts himself with a mountain deer, one with sure feet about to ascend the heights, while you or I would feel like a squashed insect beneath the weight of Habakkuk's circumstances. One will climb to the mountaintop from the valley of despair, melancholy, and desolation.

There is no better answer than Habakkuk's when faced with intolerable or unbelievable circumstances. I hope you will remember what Habakkuk's name implies, which is to wrestle if you remember nothing else from this short book, along with embrace. Sometimes we are unable to distinguish between the two.

I recall Celia, my youngest daughter, playing on a friend's backyard zip line when she was just a few years old. She smacked her face squarely against the solid trunk of the tree at the end of the rope because she was too little to prevent it. I still recall seeing blood all over her face and hearing that crack. She hit the ground senselessly and fell.

I frantically checked her pulse, which was still present, even if it wasn't as strong as I had hoped. The doctors started performing tests and doing everything they could to ensure she was okay after we took her to the emergency room. After she arrived, they tried to close the gash on the bottom of her chin. Celia, though, wasn't having it. She writhed, struggled, yelled, and continued to struggle. So, I had to restrain her.

While the doctor meticulously dressed and sewed her incisions, I did my best to keep her body and head still. It was terrible. She screamed inconsolably, "Daddy, what's happening? Please, Daddy. Please, get them to stop. I want to play. Please. I only want to have fun. Please keep them from hurting me." But I knew she needed to go through this to heal properly.

We experience these periods of kicking and screaming in our own lives. God holds and leads us through the storm even while we scream and oppose him. We want to ask him questions and demand that he respond to keep him accountable and force him to make things right away. He understands it is not feasible, though, for our own good. God must occasionally enclose us in ways that feel stiff and limiting, just as I knew I had to keep Celia down for her to heal.

Sometimes, it may seem like God is coming between us and our plans or wants, making it difficult for us or hindering our progress. We may even feel a sense of frustration or defeat that can cause us to doubt his goodness or challenge his will. But it's important to remember that God has a plan for our lives, and he loves us enough to want to protect us from anything that he believes could cause us pain.

God may be putting meaningful limits on us to provide us with special protection from the things we don't yet understand. He may be keeping us from wrong paths, situations, and decisions that could have consequences we wouldn't want to bear. Sometimes it takes us time to reflect and realize this was for our good, allowing us to become more aware and understand why God put these limits in place.

God is generous and trustworthy. He corresponds to our needs or desires with his protection to give us wisdom and discernment. His protection sometimes leads us to different paths or directions than we initially expected. He sometimes directs us to stop and slow down to become more spiritually alert and wait for further instructions regarding the path we should take to fulfill our destinies.

We must remember to seek and trust God's will in everything because he makes no mistakes. He is always working in and through us for our ultimate good, even when it may not make sense at the moment. We may not always understand why he limits us, but we can be confident knowing that God will never lead us astray. We need to be comfortable and confident in his character so that we can navigate through life with the assurance that God is always with us, and he is ultimately working all things together for our good. We must embrace and wrestle simultaneously. That is how we arrive at hope.

Chapter 17
Believe

Hope is a funny thing. When you have complete faith in God, you are filled with a sense of divine expectancy for the direction in which he is leading you. Knowing he is still in charge and on your side despite how bad things may appear gives you additional security. You also want things to change, probably in your environment but, more importantly, in your heart. The desire is to get closer to God. These two combined give you the optimism to rise above your current predicament.

According to Proverbs, "Hope deferred makes the heart sick, but a desire fulfilled is a tree of life" (13:12), and "Where there is no prophetic vision the people cast off restraint, but blessed is he who keeps the law" (29:18). Something about the ability of hope gives us energy and makes it possible for us to endure.

When you have a good reason, you can bear anything. Jesus was the best example of this. He knew the suffering he would experience when he knelt in the Garden of Gethsemane. The assaults, the beating, the jeering, the nightmare, and the embarrassment.

However, Jesus kept on going and continued to be loyal to his Father. What method did Jesus use? We have a hint from the author of the book of Hebrews.

"Looking to Jesus, the founder and perfecter of our faith, who for the joy that was set before him endured the cross, despising the shame, and is seated at the right hand of the throne of God. Consider him who endured from sinners such hostility against himself, so that you may not grow weary or fainthearted (Hebrews 12:2–3). Jesus only needed one motivation to endure the suffering. One compelling cause to stay. What motivated Him? "The joy that was set before him."

He came because of you; you were the source of his delight.

What's the purpose of carrying on when you need to know where you're heading? With hope, it is easier to leave the valley and stay there.

What do you have planned for the present day? You may enjoy a rye bread sandwich with ham and Swiss for lunch. After work, you meet a friend at your preferred coffee shop for a double espresso. You're having a birthday celebration at your sister's house this weekend and going on a beach trip the following summer. You relish the look on your child's face when they open their birthday gifts—their yearly bonus—from you.

There is nothing improper in expecting any of these. However, most of the time, the things we look forward to, expect, and aspire for are only fleeting moments of satisfaction. After all, we have more access to almost anything we want than anyone else in history. Even in January's freezing weather, are fresh peaches available? No issue. Despite your poor credit rating, can you get a vehicle loan? Many dealerships will be glad to help you. Your phone will respond when you ask for turn-by-turn directions to the party.

However, the things that mean the most typically take time—establishing devoted connections—believing in someone. Observing your children mature and obtaining a satisfying job. Sure, we may survive the day, the week, or the month on simple things.

We can only survive life with the hope of the Lord, nevertheless.

A FIRM FOUNDATION in the power that serves as the foundation for that hope, SECURITY, IS WHAT TRUE HOPE BOTH REQUIRES AND RELY ON. Before introducing the Faith Hall of Fame that we explored earlier, the author of Hebrews states "Now faith is the assurance of things hoped for, the conviction of things not seen," (Hebrews 11:1). But we are all aware of how challenging it may be to act on our faith when there are no clear justifications. As a result, by its definition, faith appears to be doing something for which there is no rational justification. And if God's nature—and our relationship with him—doesn't serve as our foundation, we might as well put our faith in the North Pole or our iPhone.

God is more precise than anything else in our lives, regardless of what we see and feel. And I'm aware that these impersonal thoughts and notions may begin to be perplexing or appear far from the struggles you may face with real-world issues like bills and bankruptcy. However, Scripture defines their relationship in the following way: "Not only that, but we rejoice in our sufferings, knowing that suffering produces endurance, and endurance produces character, and character produces hope, and hope does not put us to shame, because God's love has been poured into our hearts through the Holy Spirit who has been given to us (Romans 5:3–5)."

My perspective on this transition from pain to closeness with God is as follows: When we are going through a difficult moment, we take God at his word and trust that he is still in charge and has a plan. So, relying on him, we continue. We get stronger as we persevere, hour by hour, day by day, and week by week. Our faith, maturity, and trust in God all increase as we age. When we are more resilient, our faith is in God's kindness rather than our current situation. We learn to trust God's promises rather than our senses.

God will visit you amid your efforts if you still want to believe. God will recognize the enthusiasm and sincerity of your desire, even if you hurl your Bible across the room, as Anthony Graves did, shake your fist at him, as Habakkuk did, or doubt him. God will walk beside you in every step if you truly want to feel his love and care for you while you go through trials—if you want that more than you expect, your circumstances will improve, and your comfort will return.

I am aware that this journey of faith is easier said than done. And as we've seen, it's often a matter of perspective. I have a little poem that will help you emphasize this topic. William Nguyen, a young person from our church, wrote these verses when he was fifteen:

The journey of faith it's easier said than done,
We set out on a quest to God in the battle we've won.
It takes strength, courage, a steadfast will
We must be mindful of our faith, seizing every moment to fulfill.
The roads are long, often filled with trials
But God is there, gently guiding all our smiles.
We falter, stumble, and fail
But when we cry out, he hears us wail.
When we take his hand, it is an ageless bond
We can't give up, and we must carry on.
So, do not fear the struggles down this way,
For God is with us, and life is made for today.
With courage and trust, journeys will be complete
God will bring joy to our souls in blissful replete.

AHEM...

Hey there!

So, you know that feeling you get when you find your new favorite thing and you just HAVE to shout it from the mountaintops to anyone who has the ears to hear? Of course you do! You've read "God or Bust: How to Keep the Faith When Life Knocks You Down," and now it's your chance to be the hero of the Amazon review section.

Did the book make you laugh, cry, or even do a little happy dance? Did it make you stare off into space while sipping your favorite cup of coffee? Whatever it made you feel, by all means, spill the beans (pun in-ten-ded).

Your honest review will not only help other readers decide if this book is *their* cup of tea (or coffee), but it'll also make the author do his own happy dance. And let's be real, who doesn't love the idea of making someone's day AND spreading a little literary love?

So, after you read the conclusion, summon your inner critic (or cheerleader), and let the world know what you thought of this book. Spoiler alert: Your words could be the reason someone discovers their new favorite read!

Cheers,

Jason C. Johnson Sr.

Conclusion

To Doubt or to Believe?

This wasn't supposed to happen! Vincent, Melissa's brother, had been admitted to the hospital on Christmas Eve due to breathing issues. His doctor wanted to ensure that his severe cold didn't turn into pneumonia or something more serious. They were aware, as were we all, that her brother, who was 34 years old, was prone to illnesses of all types due to his weakened immune system.

He stayed in the hospital after a week and showed no signs of improvement. A few days later, everything started to go south for him. Of course, Melissa, I, and our family were praying the entire time. But now we all called everyone we knew to ask for prayer support. I contacted my pastor friends and their congregations worldwide, pleading with them to pray for our loved ones.

I felt God would use Vincent in extraordinary ways because of his grand narrative. Vincent had rediscovered Christ after emerging from a life of suffering and rebellion. Since then, he has grown into a magnificent man of God, a godly husband, a father, and a worship leader. Vincent had the deepest love for God and wanted to share his experience with others, so they would be inspired that God could (and would) help them through their troubles.

God must be able to heal such a strong ambassador, right? As yet another week came and went, we kept on praying. One moment, tens of thousands of people were thought to be praying for Vincent's recovery throughout the world. God would heal my brother-in-law, and I knew it. He didn't, though.

A few days later, Vincent passed away. We were all in shock. None of us had expected God to respond the way he had.

I helped preach at Vincent's funeral, as hard as it was. I can't begin to express how upsetting it was to see my wife's and our entire family's eyes filled with tears. We were aware that we might never be able to grasp why God had not granted our requests fully. But even amid our sorrow, we were thankful that God had welcomed Vincent home. I decided to share the gospel while feeling that peculiar mixture of sadness and gratitude. That's what Vincent would have wanted. And that's what our God would have preferred, too.

I wanted to spread the gospel of God's grace and the atoning work of Jesus on the cross because I knew many extended family members would be there, including some who rarely attended church. As awful and illogical as Vincent's passing appeared, I wanted to do all in my power to make sure that it triggered others to consider their relationship with God.

And God made a strong move. Many people decided to place their complete trust in Jesus on that day. It wasn't just their anguish over losing Vincent that was causing it. In that service, the Holy Spirit was clearly at work and impossible to miss. Although it didn't lessen our sorrow over losing Vincent, there was great comfort in knowing that God was using his life and death to point people to Christ and have a profoundly positive impact on everyone there.

I tell you this story because it's one of the most straightforward and moving times I've ever experienced, experiencing the kind of faith we've been discussing in Habakkuk, the kind that welcomes and wrestles, the type that doubts God while still trusting him. Even though I miss Vincent being here with us, I can't deny that God has used his passing to bring many others to himself, individuals who otherwise would not have heard and listened to the gospel.

Melissa remarked that she missed her brother several years later. We had a long conversation about it, and I asked her something that had been in my heart for a while. I said, "We can both agree that God touched so many lives through Vincent's life and death." She gave the nod in agreement. "But Melissa, would you make that trade if we could have him back with us here on earth in exchange for giving up all the good God accomplished?"

Melissa responded without hesitating. "One day, thanks to what God carried out through Vincent, I will meet Vincent and many more people again in heaven. The good of God's design has never changed."

We both started crying and thanked God that his ways were higher than ours. I don't know what you've been through or are going through. And we are still waiting to be made aware of what will await us tomorrow. But I know this: our God is a good God who loved us enough to provide the best gift he could give—his beloved Son—so that we can know him, praise him on earth, and spend eternity with him in heaven.

He cares for us so deeply. Only because he first loved us can we love him or anybody else (1 John 4:19). When difficult circumstances arise, and your best response is to wish to believe, that is sufficient. Continue to desire to believe. Trust that God is standing by you and let that glimmer of hope develop. Ask God to help you in overcoming your unbelief in prayer, just like the possessed boy's father did. Ask your questions as Habakkuk did, and then be ready to hear God's reply.

The book of Habakkuk only includes three brief chapters, as you may have seen. First, Habakkuk expresses skepticism, and he waits in the second. He is accepting God's goodness in the third. As you mature, you will have the kind of faith shown by Habakkuk in Chapter 3. You can't have the faith described in Chapter 3 unless you've experienced Chapter 1's questioning and Chapter 2's waiting. God works more in the valley than on the mountaintop.

Instead of trying to run back and retrace their steps to some former peak, those closest to God have leaned into the trials and wrestled with God, questioning him, yet trusting that he is good and that he will use everything to carry out his purposes. He will bring them back out better, stronger, and more intimately connected to him than ever. They understand that, in the end, this process will prove God's faithfulness, character, goodness, and love.

Not all of your questions and answers are available to me. But now that I have been loving God and following Christ for over 29 years, I can confidently claim that I have spent enough time with Jesus to trust him with all of my tomorrows. I genuinely hope and pray that you feel that same assurance, as easy as that may sound. If not right away, then very soon.

Do you want to draw closer to God? Do you value your relationship with him more than a pleasant, trouble-free life? Do you want to know that no matter what is happening to you, he is there for you and cares about you? Then, by God's grace and with his strength, do not doubt and never give up!

Nobody's life is perfect. When tough times come, it can be difficult to keep a positive outlook and to see the silver lining in life's challenges. The sun might not appear shining when we face our troubles and feel like there is no escape. However, that doesn't mean we must give in to despair.

No matter how bleak a situation or how insurmountable the challenges we are facing may appear, optimism is still possible with a little effort. We can start by remembering those dark moments are usually transient and will pass eventually. Life offers difficulties, hardships, and obstacles, but we will make it through if we keep our chin up and focus on the light ahead.

In addition, it can help us take small but meaningful actions to lift our spirits. Connecting with family and friends and engaging our senses by doing things we enjoy, such as taking a walk, playing music, reading, writing, or even just taking some time to sit and daydream, can all be powerful means of restoring a sense of optimism and hope.

Lastly, it is important to understand that going through the darkness and coming out on the other side is normal and necessary. We will never arrive at a place of perfect contentment and peace. Still, if we persist, surround ourselves with positivity, and keep our gaze forward, we will eventually get to a place where things feel easier.

In short, optimism is not a naïve outlook or a naïve wish for life to be how we would like it to be. It is just a way of looking at the world and ourselves from a place of resilience and hope. Amidst the turmoil, it can be hard to remain optimistic, but if we keep up the effort, this outlook can be a powerful remedy against life's most difficult moments.

When we face trying times, it can feel like the walls are closing in around us and we cannot find lasting peace or strength. But the secret to facing these trials with courage and resilience is to turn to God. God's love, faithfulness, and grace are unending sources of hope. He is there for us in every difficult season and will never turn us away. He has the power and ability to pull us through any circumstances and bring us back to the safety of his provision.

The more we seek God, the more we begin to understand the depths of his grace, mercy, and love, which are unparalleled and boundless. A relationship built with the Lord will reshape our thoughts and outlook on life. Having a personal relationship with him helps put aside our insecurities, worries, and anxieties and lets us rely on his strength to face and overcome obstacles. His grace continuously works within us to build courage, faith, and trust in him, which can help get us past any struggles.

Turning to God is a sure way to find the hope, strength, and refuge we look for. Having faith in him offers anchoring security and peace that cannot be found in anything else. No matter how bad things are for us, he is our advocate and friend always in the way. By growing in the Lord and opening up to his incredible grace, we can be sure of his love, trust and protection.

Sometimes it is difficult to have faith in God. We all pass through days or even years when everything feels hopeless and not right without an obvious explanation. But there's a source of optimism, faith, and hope we can hold onto while the world crumbles around us: It is God.

God is forever faithful as a loving Father who never leaves us alone. In whichever situation he always stands with us though it may involve raising us up after falling down or bringing us back whenever we lose focus. He is still the fountain of our everlasting hope; he will never let go of us even if everything else does so too. The knowledge that we can rely on him at all times gives us the strength to face hard moments with courage.

We can live confidently knowing that God will not leave us behind but will love us during every form adversity experienced by his people. No matter what comes our way, we see that God's protective covering over our lives filled with undeserved kindnesses and guidance in our spiritual journeys throughout life. His commitment to us never changes, unlike the false delusions promised by this world; he doesn't fail because his word has gone out concerning this fact already! Trusting him means that life doesn't have to be terrifying anymore because he will remain true to his promises despite the difficulties we face.

Hope comes from God alone who is certain about things for which there is no visible basis whatsoever. Even in tough times like these when one looks around, they don't see any light at the end of a tunnel or know where to find their creator when they need him most. He always stands firm beside me whether I find myself in a bad situation or not and is always ready to guide me into the right path. Through our trials, we grow stronger and become more courageous as we keep believing and trusting in God. In every situation, God will be faithful to us; he will never forsake nor leave us alone even during the darkest days when it seems like all other avenues are closed for existence itself. The future that looks promising comes from him; it is the darkness that humankind has seen.

Life can be unbearable at times so that one feels surrounded by darkness on all sides. We may feel discouraged or lose patience with ourselves, especially if there are difficult moments when no one else around us understands what we face. However, if we turn to God's unending love and grace, we can get through this season with hope.

We can rely on him because he is always dependable. God said I will never leave you nor forsake you. Even when things appear hopeless and as though he has left us completely abandoned, he still remains present within our lives. We must try to search him out. An earnest prayer can do wonders. Turning to God as my stronghold gives me faith that he hears me whenever I cry unto Him

Building a relationship with God has been made possible through conscious effort on our part. But fear not! Having an honest heart before his presence allows him to receive us with open arms. Feeding on his Word builds spiritual life within, brings joy overflowing into my being while reminding me of who he is consistently good & unchanging towards man.

In times of great distress, we should always remember that God is still good, and his love stretches far beyond what we can see. By beginning every morning with a declaration of God's goodness and faithfulness and ending each night in thanksgiving and surrender, we can choose to be optimistic and hopeful in the light of his mercy. With God by our side, there is always a reason to live life with purpose and to find happiness even in the midst of the most challenging circumstances.

REFERENCES

Blackaby, H. T., & Blackaby, M. (2009). Experiencing the spirit: The power of Pentecost every day. Multnomah.

Chambers, O. (1976). Daily thoughts for disciples. Zondervan Publishing Company.

Gesenius, W. F. (1979). Gesenius's Hebrew and chaldee lexicon to the Old Testament scriptures, TR., with additions and corrections from the author's other works, by S.P. Tregelles (S. P. Tregelles, Trans.) (7th ed.). Baker Pub Group.

Godin, S. (2007). The dip: A little book that teaches you when to quit (and when to stick). Penguin.

God's faithfulness in providing. (2016, July 7). GeorgeMuller.org.

Graves, A. (2018). Infinite hope: How wrongful conviction, solitary confinement, and 12 years on death row failed to kill my soul. Beacon Press.

Lewis, C. S. (2001). The problem of pain. Zondervan.

Lewis, C. S. (2009). Mere Christianity. HarperCollins.

Yancey, P. (2010). Where is God when it hurts? Zondervan.

Next Read

Did you love God or Bust: How to Keep the Faith When Life Knocks You Down? Then you should read ***The 40 Day Fire: Burn Away Every Obstacle to Your Destiny*** by

Jason C. Johnson Sr.!

The 40 Day Fire

The 40 Day Fire is a 40-day journey intended to light a fire underneath you! From time to time, all of us need a little push. This book will sometimes cause you to laugh and at other times will lovingly give you a kick in the pants to help you to stay on course. The author's intention: help you to burn away everything in your life that is currently standing in the way between you and your destiny. Life, no matter how long one has to live it, is relatively short. Every human being has a purpose to fulfill in this life but distractions, which come at us a mile a minute, make it difficult for us to stay focused and motivated. ***The 40 Day Fire*** will help you to keep your heart and mind in line with whom God has created you to be and with the vision that he has given to you, and only you, to fulfill.

ABOUT THE PUBLISHER

One Plan Media LLC provides quality content in book publications, sound recordings, film and audiobook productions. You can find all of the newest releases at https://linktr.ee/oneplanmedia

One Plan Media also provides voice-over narration and publishing services for a wide range of creative projects. If you would like to submit your manuscript to One Plan Media for a publishing deal or to produce an audiobook or video, please send all queries to info.oneplanmedia@gmail.com or scan the QR code above.

www.ingramcontent.com/pod-product-compliance
Lightning Source LLC
Chambersburg PA
CBHW030524080526
44586CB00011B/313